Dialectical + Acceptance & Commitment Therapy Workbook: 50+ DBT & ACT Skills & Guided Mindfulness Meditations For Emotional Intelligence, Anxiety, Depression, OCD & Overthinking

Contents

Introduction

It is natural for individuals to be in pain. Suffering, on the other hand, may not always imply bodily or psychological agony. People also have to deal with negative self-evaluations, unpleasant sensations, and traumatic memories. We do everything we can to prevent pain because we dread or worry about it. We wish to keep our pain to a minimum. Feeling healthier is something that many of us appreciate highly. However, a good life entails much more than the absence of sorrow. We want to enjoy our brief time on this world and make the most of it. Acceptance and Commitment Therapy (ACT) is a type of psychotherapy that focuses on the subject of human suffering, but it also extends beyond that. It's also about appreciating human sorrow as a necessary component of living well. This new type of Cognitive Behavioral Therapy (CBT) concentrates on big topics such "What is my ultimate purpose in life?"

Chapter 1
Acceptance and Commitment therapy: What to know

Acceptance and commitment therapy, or ACT, is a type of psychotherapy that incorporates mindfulness and cognitive behavioral therapy. Because it encourages patients to participate in values-based beneficial actions even while they are experiencing unpleasant sensations, feelings, or ideas, it is also known as contextual psychotherapy. To put it another way, it aids patients in developing psychological flexibility.

Mindfulness, dispersing difficult ideas, and tolerating unpleasant sensations are all emphasized in ACT. With ACT, you'll learn to detach yourself from your ideas, which will lead to a more meaningful existence. Your efforts are founded on your commitment to establishing your ideals via action.

ACT breaks mindfulness skills down into 3 categories:

1) Defusion: distancing from, and letting go of, unhelpful thoughts, beliefs and memories

2) Acceptance: making room for painful feelings, urges and sensations, and allowing them to come and go without a struggle

3) Contact with the present moment: engaging fully with your here-and-now experience, with an attitude of openness and curiosity

ACT can be delivered in many different ways:

Brief - ACT is completed in only four one-hour sessions.

Medium-term - ACT takes eight hours to complete.

Long-term ACT - ACT consists of forty two-hour sessions.

Experiential psychotherapy (ACT)

ACT is a relatively new type of cognitive behavioral therapy that has received a lot of attention in recent years. It promotes principles, acceptance, awareness, and practices that assist people in overcoming obstacles in their lives.

A fundamental assumption of ACT is that human pain is a normal and unavoidable part of being human. It's also about individuals trying to control or avoid their own experiences, which may lead to human misery and other parts of our life that don't function. ACT can assist patients in learning effective pain management techniques, practicing mindfulness, gaining insight about what actually matters, and seeking a more meaningful existence. The purpose of ACT is to learn how to live life without too much strain, not to get rid of pain.

Because its researchers and practitioners are dedicated to the promotion of science and the empirical study of its causes and effects, ACT is termed empirical psychotherapy.

My Coping Strategies

Please list a few of the ways you have been coping with your difficult thoughts and feelings:	Does this strategy work in the short term? Do you feel better?	Does this strategy work in the long term? Do the difficult thoughts and feelings show up again?	Does this strategy have any negative consequences or cause any problems of its own? Does it help you live a better life?

If any of these coping skills are working for you and aren't causing their own problems, keep using them! If any of them are not working or are creating other problems for you, this toolkit will offer you some alternative skills to try.

The Basics of ACT

The following activity will assist you in grasping the key ideas of the ACT method. When you feel something, it's sometimes simpler to understand than when someone attempts to describe it to you in words. While reading the following exercise, try to follow the directions as closely as possible. It's very normal to become distracted or lose attention. When you sense your thoughts drifting, simply refocus on the workout.

Please locate a comfortable position in your chair where you can sit for 5 to 10 minutes while remaining reasonably motionless. I recommend putting your feet on the floor and folding your arms over your legs or in your lap, but you may do whatever feels best to you.

Take a mental scan of your entire body from head to toe... Check to see if any regions of your body are tense, such as your jaw or shoulders... If you're feeling tense, consider letting go of part of it... If not, that's great; just take note of what's around you.

Spend a few time getting to know your sense of touch... Pay attention to the bodily feelings that develop in your hands... Check to see if you can detect where your hands and legs come into touch... Check to see whether you can feel your toes on the ground...

After then, spend a few seconds to really listen to what you're hearing... It might be a series of noises, a single sound, or nothing at all. Simply take note of everything that is present...

Focus your attention on your breathing when you're ready... Observe how the breath enters and exits on its own, without your intervention... Check to see whether you can sense your breath in your nose or belly button...

You will notice that when you breathe, thoughts will arise in your head... They might be either pleasant or painful, or neutral ideas... The human mind is a thinking machine, and it performs just this... Simply attempt to observe your thoughts without becoming engrossed in them, and then return your focus to your breathing... Whenever a thought arises, acknowledge it and then return your focus to your breathing... This will happen repeatedly, which is fine since it implies you are typical... You may improve your ability to notice your thoughts rather of allowing them to lead you away with practice.

You'll notice that as you continue to breathe, various sentiments or emotions may arise... These sensations might be joyful, bad, or indifferent... Try to pay attention to these sensations in the same way you pay attention to your ideas... You don't have to strive to modify what's already there; simply pay attention to how you feel... When you sense a sensation, attempt to pinpoint its location in your body... Pay attention to the feelings that go along with the emotion... Heaviness, lightness, warmth, coldness, tingling, or tension are all possibilities... These feelings might be felt in your head, shoulders, arms, legs, or abdomen...

Whatever you're feeling and whatever occurs, simply pay attention to it and try to let it go...

And now attempt to return your focus to your breathing... Try to notice that you have a part of you that can monitor your breathing, your thoughts, your feelings, and the sensations that are occurring in your body... There's a part of you that thinks and feels, and another that can detect the thinking and feeling... Allow yourself a few seconds to feel what it's like to connect with the part of you that only sees...

Now take a few seconds to consider what has got you to this point... There's something so important to you that you've made the effort to come here... Consider for a moment what is most important to you in your life... Recognize and celebrate the fact that you have chosen to make a difference... After you've completed the practice, imagine yourself as the sort of person you want to be when you've properly dealt with your suffering... Consider how you will interact with others... and how you will interact with yourself...

When you're ready, carefully return your focus to the room and to where we are right now. You can stretch and move your fingers and toes if you like.

Weekly Evaluation Sheet

On a scale from 0 to 100, how well is your life working?

Date →													
Scale ↓	The way I'm spending each day makes me feel alive and fulfilled												
100													
95													
90													
85													
80													
75													
70													
65													
60													

55												
50												
45												
40												
35												
30												
25												
20												
15												
10												
5												
0												
	The way I'm spending each day makes life seem pointless, meaningless, and not worth living at all											

Exercise 1: Past, present, and future

#1

Please use the Weekly Evaluation Sheet to assess how well your life is doing.

#2

How have the mindfulness and defusion exercises gone for you?

What did you take away from either of the articles about mindfulness if you read them?

What thoughts or feelings were getting in the way if you didn't execute any of the exercises?

#3

Main concepts:

1. Negative thoughts and sentiments about the past or future cause pain and suffering.

2. The present moment is a secure space with which we may connect at any time.

3. When we practice being in the now, we are less influenced by unpleasant ideas and feelings about the past or the future.

4. Connecting with the present is about having the flexibility to make choices that enhance our lives, not about controlling how we think and feel.

#4

Practicing new abilities:

To experience the process of present awareness, please select one of the following alternatives. When you experience something for yourself rather than having someone try to explain it to you in words, it is sometimes simpler to grasp. When you're listening to the activity, try to follow the directions as closely as possible. Don't be concerned if you become distracted or lose your concentration. That is very natural. When you sense your thoughts drifting, simply refocus on the workout.

#5

Between now and the following module, when you're ready...

To help you connect with the current moment, please pick one or more of the following methods:

A raisin experiment in mindful eating.

Take a handful of raisins and hold them in your hand. You can substitute anything different if you don't have raisins.

Assume you've recently arrived on Earth from a faraway planet where you didn't have access to such cuisine. Now that you have this meal in your hands, you may begin to examine it with all of your senses, focusing on one of the things as if it were the first time you had seen it. Concentrate on observing that thing. Scrutinize everything and investigate every detail as though you've never seen anything like it before. Rotate it with your fingers and see which color it is. Look for creases and areas where the surface reflects or darkens light.

After that, feel the texture to see if it's soft, hard, rough, or smooth. If you're thinking to yourself, "Why am I performing this strange exercise?" If you're thinking, "How is this going to benefit me?" or "I despise these items," just notice them, let them go, and return your focus to the object.

Place the thing in your nose and take note of how it smells. Bring the object up to one of your ears, squeeze it, roll it about, and listen to see if it makes a sound.

Start by bringing the thing to your lips slowly. Take note of how your arm understands where it belongs, and how your mouth moist as you eat. When you're ready to swallow, become aware of your desire to do so. Then, when you swallow the raisin and feel it slide down your throat and through your esophagus on its trip to your stomach, try to observe the sensations.

Give yourself a pat on the back for taking the time to eat thoughtfully.

The Observing Self (Exercise 2)

#1

Please rate how well your life is operating using the Weekly Assessment Sheet.

#2

How did the present-moment mindfulness exercises go for you?

What thoughts or sentiments came in the way if you didn't execute any of the exercises?

#3

Key concepts:

1. We have a part of ourselves that thinks, a portion that feels, and a part of ourselves that can notice and observe our thinking and feelings.

The Observing Self, the Perceiving Self, the Observing Self, Pure Awareness, or any other term that makes sense to us might be given to this portion of ourselves.

3. The Observing Self is a secure space with which we can connect at any moment.

4. Our ideas and feelings have less power over us when we connect with our Observing Self.

5. Connecting with our Observing Self is about having the flexibility to make choices that enhance our lives, not about controlling how we think and feel.

#4

Put your new talents to the test:

Please try one of the tasks below to get a feel for the process of connecting with the observing self. When you experience something for yourself rather than having someone try to explain it to you in words, it is sometimes simpler to grasp. When you're listening to the activity, try to follow the directions as closely as possible. Don't be concerned if you become distracted or lose your concentration. That is very natural. When you sense your thoughts drifting, simply refocus on the workout.

#5

Between now and the following module, when you're ready...

Please put down your commitment to doing one of the aforementioned exercises a particular number of times. Between now and the following module, you can complete the exercise once a day, once every two days, or simply once. It's all up to you. Simply attempt to practice as much as you have promised. Don't be concerned if you don't meet your target.

We don't aim for perfection; instead, we do our best. Continue to the next module regardless of what occurs. Difficult emotions and sentiments can sometimes interfere with our life and prevent us from accomplishing our goals. That's perfectly typical! And that's exactly what we're working on in these activities.

Chapter 2
Acceptance & Commitment Therapy vs Cognitive Behavioral Therapy

CBT examines a person's compulsion-inducing distorted mental processes. Problematic beliefs are not tested in ACT. Rather, it encourages a person to alter his or her standards and the meaning he or she assigns to troublesome viewpoints, making them less frightening and exciting to the individual. CBT focuses on creating strategies for coping with unpleasant ideas, actions, and emotions. CBT aims to provide conflict resolution and pressure reduction strategies. Furthermore, CBT focuses primarily on the cognitive constructions that cause emotions. As a result, people try to alter or replace the thinking. ACT, on the other hand, does not place a premium on emotional regulation. Feelings should instead be experienced and re-experienced, recognized but not stressed. ACT also places a strong emphasis on self-awareness and value orientation.

ACT focuses on the mind's most crucial problem-solving mode, to which literal language and logic appear to easily lead.

Theory of Relational Frames

The essential premise of ACT is framed by Relational Frame Theory (RFT). The goal of RFT is to investigate the relationship between human behavior and language.

The mind and language

Words, sights, sounds, facial emotions, and bodily gestures are all part of human language, which is a very sophisticated system of symbols. Humans utilize language in both public and private settings. Speaking, talking, facial expressions, gestures, writing, drawing, sculpting, singing, dancing, acting, and so on are all examples of public language use. Thinking, envisioning, daydreaming, planning, picturing, analysing, brooding, fantasizing, and so on are examples of private language usage. (The term cognition is frequently used to describe the use of private language.)

The mind, of course, is neither a "thing" or a "object." The term "mind" refers to a vast array of interconnected cognitive activities such as analysing, comparing, evaluating, planning, remembering, imagining, and so on. And all of these intricate processes are dependent on the sophisticated system of symbols known as human language. As a result, when we use the term "mind" on ACT, we're referring to "human language."

While human language has several benefits, it may also have drawbacks. We use language to make biased and cruel beliefs about the people around us, to construct negative ideas, to feel outraged about things, and to relive previous traumas. Overuse of words and thought can also lead to a loss of awareness of the current moment. We might spend so much time ruminating on the past and fretting about the future that we forget to appreciate the present.

The model of psychological adaptability

The basic purpose of ACT is to develop our psychological flexibility, or our capacity to stay present as a fully conscious human being and, depending on the circumstances, maintain or adjust our behavior to serve chosen ideals.

Simply expressed, this implies we should be more aware of our own emotions and ideas, and connect our conduct with long-term ideals rather than fleeting sentiments, thoughts, and impulses.

Emotions and beliefs are notoriously poor markers of long-term worth. They are difficult to control and have a proclivity for going to extremes. Allowing our emotions and ideas to affect our actions may cause us to miss out on more significant emerging patterns in action, preventing us from discerning true meaning in our lives or experiencing life's richness.

What is ACT's purpose?

In layman's words, the purpose of ACT is to live a full, satisfying, and meaningful life while embracing the sorrow that comes with it. Why is it that suffering is an unavoidable part of life? When we are confronted with difficult ideas, feelings, or sensations, we all too frequently behave in ways that are ultimately self-defeating or harmful. As a result, teaching patients how to effectively manage pain via mindfulness activities is a crucial part of ACT.

What is mindfulness, exactly?

"Mindfulness" is an old idea found in Buddhism, Taoism, Hinduism, Judaism, Islam, and Christianity, among other historic spiritual and religious traditions. The various advantages of practicing mindfulness abilities have just lately been recognized in Western psychology. If you read a few books on the subject, you'll notice that the term "mindfulness" is defined in many different ways, yet they all boil down to the same thing:

Listening with flexibility, openness, and curiosity is what mindfulness entails.

This straightforward definition conveys three key points. First and foremost, mindfulness is an awareness rather than a cognitive process. Rather of getting "caught up" in your thoughts, it's about bringing your focus to your current reality. Second, mindfulness necessitates a particular mindset: one of openness and inquiry. Even if your current experience is tough, painful, or unsettling, you may remain open and interested about it rather than avoiding or combating it. Finally, mindfulness entails attention flexibility: the ability to deliberately direct, extend, or focus your attention on various areas of your experience.

Mindfulness may help us "wake up," connect with ourselves, and enjoy the depth of each moment. It may be used to improve our self-awareness, allowing us to understand more about how we feel, think, and behave. We may utilize them to form deep and intimate connections with others we care about, including ourselves. We may also utilize it to actively control our own behavior and broaden our variety of responses to the environment around us. It's the art of living mindfully, and it's a powerful approach to boost psychological resilience and improve life pleasure.

Of course, there's a lot more to ACT than mindfulness. It's also about living an appreciating lifestyle: persistent activity that is linked with basic beliefs. In fact, at ACT, we teach mindfulness techniques with the explicit goal of supporting valued action: assisting individuals in living their values. In other words, the goal of ACT is to help people live more aware, useful lives. This will become obvious in the following section, which examines ACT's six key processes.

ACT's six main therapeutic procedures

Contacting the present moment, defusion, acceptance, self-context, values, and engaged action are the six main therapeutic processes of ACT.

Getting in touch with the present moment (being here now).

Being psychologically present, or contacting the present moment, is intentionally connecting with and participating with what is happening right now. Staying present is quite challenging for us as humans. We know how easy it is to become lost in our thoughts and lose contact with the world around us, just like everyone else. We may be distracted with ideas about the past or the future for long periods of time. Alternatively, we may not be completely conscious of our sensations and instead "go about our day" on autopilot. Getting in touch with the present moment entails being able to focus our attention on either the physical world around us or the psychological world within us, or both at the same time. It also entails intentionally attending to our present reality rather than wandering off into our thoughts or operating on "autopilot."

Defusion

Learning to "take a step back" and detach or disengage from our thoughts, images, and memories is referred to as defusion. (The technical name is "cognitive defusion," although we commonly refer to it as "defusion.") We let them come and go as if they were merely automobiles passing in front of our house, rather than getting caught up in them or allowing them to push us about. Rather than becoming tied up in our ideas, we take a step back and examine them. We view our thoughts for what they are: words or pictures, nothing more or less. Instead of gripping them hard, we hold them softly.

Acceptance (opening up) is allowing and making room for unpleasant feelings, sensations, desires, and emotions. We stop battling with them, give them space to breathe, and let them be themselves. Rather than battling, opposing, fleeing, or being overwhelmed by them, we open up to them and allow them to be. (Note:

This does not imply that we like or desire them.) It just implies that we make room for them!)

The Self as a Setting (Pure Awareness)

We talk of the "mind" in common English without comprehending that it is made up of two different elements: the thinking self and the watching self. The thinking self, or the part of ourselves that is continuously thinking and forming ideas, beliefs, memories, judgements, fantasies, plans, and so on, is something we are all quite familiar with. The watching self, on the other hand, is a part of ourselves that is aware of what we are thinking, feeling, perceiving, or doing at any particular time. "Pure consciousness" is another phrase for this. The technical word at ACT is "self-context." Your body, ideas, feelings, and roles change with time, but the "you" who is able to perceive or observe all of these things remains constant. It's the same "you" who's been there your entire life. Rather of using the technical phrase "self as context," we call it "the observing self" when we communicate to our clients.

Values (understanding what matters).

What do you want to achieve in your life from the bottom of your heart? What is it that you wish to be known for? What are your plans for your limited time on our planet? In the broad scheme of things, what is most essential to you? Values are traits that people want to see in their actions. To put it another way, they describe how we wish to act all of the time. Clarifying one's values is a necessary first step in living a meaningful life. Values are frequently referred to as "selected life path" at ACT.

Values are frequently compared to a compass because they provide direction and guidance.

Dedicated action (Do what is necessary).

Committed action is doing successful action while being true to our principles. Knowing our values is great, but life becomes richer, fuller, and more meaningful only when we behave in ways that are consistent with our beliefs. In other words, if we merely gaze at the compass, we won't travel very far; we'll only get far if we move our arms and legs in the direction we want to go. Value-driven activity elicits a wide range of emotions and ideas, both good and bad, joyful and painful. As a result, committed action means that we "do whatever it takes" to live our ideals, even if it entails suffering. All classic behavioral therapy techniques, such as goal setting, exposure, behavioral activation, and skills training, can be applied in this section of the model. And every skill that enhances and enriches life may be taught in this part, from negotiating to time management, assertiveness to problem solving, self-soothing to crisis management.

A six-sided diamond represents psychological flexibility.

Keep in mind that ACT's six main processes are not distinct from one another. Although we refer to them in this fashion for practical reasons—to assist therapists and clients in learning and using the ACT model—more it's intuitive to conceive of them as six facets of a diamond. The diamond itself is a symbol of psychological adaptability.

Psychological flexibility is the ability to be fully aware of and open to our experiences in the present moment, driven by our ideals. It's the capacity to "be present, open up, and do what counts," to put it another way. The basic purpose of ACT is to develop psychological flexibility on a technical level. The greater our quality of life, the better we are able to be fully conscious, open to our experiences, and act on our principles, since we can respond much more effectively to the issues and challenges that life inevitably presents. We create a feeling of purpose and enjoy a sense of energy when we are completely involved in our lives and guided by our ideals.

As indicated below, the above essential processes may be divided into three functional parts. Detaching from ideas and feelings, recognizing them for what they are, giving them space, and allowing them to come and go on their own are all part of defusion and acceptance. To put it another way, "opening up." Getting in touch with the present moment and self as context (also known as the watching self) both require getting in touch with verbal and nonverbal parts of your here-and-now experience. To put it another way, "being present." The efficient use of language to facilitate life-enhancing activity is at the heart of values and engaged action. To put it another way, "doing what matters." The capacity to "be present, open up, and do what counts" is referred to as psychological flexibility.

The abbreviation ACT

The complete model is summarized by a simple acronym, which you should regularly share with your clients.

Accept your thoughts and feelings, and be present.

ACT:

A = Accept your thoughts and feelings, and be present.

C = Pick a worthwhile path.

T stands for "take action."

Chapter 3
Setting goals with Acceptance and Commitment therapy

Setting objectives based on values is encouraged by ACT. It consists of three major steps:

1. Decide which aspect of your life you wish to improve.

Community, love, education, career, personal growth, environment, family, parenting, health, money, and more are all examples of this.

2. Create SMART goals that are precise, measurable, adaptive, realistic, and time-bound.

Try to be as detailed as possible when describing what you intend to achieve. Make sure you understand the procedures necessary to complete the task. A precise aim is more manageable than a broad goal. If you only establish a goal to spend more time with your child, for example, you have no way of knowing if you've actually accomplished it. A more precise objective is to spend at least one hour each day playing with your youngster. If you establish a clear goal for yourself, you'll be able to identify if you've met it and track your progress appropriately.

Meaningful - Consider if your aim is actually founded on your beliefs, rather than merely a set of rules or a sense of obligation. If you don't believe your objectives have a deeper significance, consider whether they are truly impacted by the values that matter to you. Remember that your primary values should be founded on things that give your life significance.

Adaptable - Make sure your objective helps you progress in the direction you feel will benefit your life the most. Examine if your objective is bringing you closer to or further away from your life's ultimate purpose.

Realistic - If you create objectives that are not genuinely reachable, you are likely to experience disappointment, frustration, and failure. Attempt to strike a balance between goals that are relatively simple to attain and those that are nearly hard to achieve. Be practical and realistic.

Period-bound - Define your objectives even more precisely by specifying a time and date by which you intend to attain them. If this isn't possible or reasonable, attempt to establish a deadline for yourself and do everything you can to stick to it.

3. Determine the importance of your objectives.

The third stage is to choose how quickly you want to attain your objective. Your objectives might be as follows:

Long-term - Make a list of actions you'll need to perform over the next six months to a year to move closer to your goals.

Medium-term - Think about the steps you'll need to take in the next two to three months to move closer to your objectives.

Short-term - Make a list of the tasks you'll need to complete in the next month to achieve your objectives.

Immediately - What are the objectives you need to meet in the next week or perhaps the next day?

It will drive your committed behaviors if you begin to live in accordance with your unique fundamental principles. Our finest goals and values are meaningless unless they are backed up by action. Knowing what basic principles you actually wish to pursue might help you live a life of significance.

Chapter 4
Overcoming Post traumatic stress disorder with Activities

You may acquire post-traumatic stress disorder if you have encountered or seen a surprising, scary, or hazardous incident. These traumatic incidents might include everything from a house fire to the death of a loved one to surviving a car accident. The more terror, helplessness, serious damage, or death an experience awakens, the more severe the PTSD.

PTSD's main signs and symptoms

Re-experiencing symptoms refers to a person's mental re-enactment of a traumatic incident. The person may have flashbacks of the terrible incident, such as losing their home in a fire that killed a loved one. Traumatic experiences make a person feel helpless, and when they resurface as flashbacks or intrusive thoughts, the individual feels depleted. After repeating the horrible occurrence in their mind's eye, they are unable to deal with the remainder of the day.

Symptoms of avoidance: People with PTSD prefer to avoid circumstances or activities that remind them of their traumatic occurrence. For example, if a loved one died in a boating accident that capsized, they may deliberately avoid ever going into another boat. This is because they would have no piece of mind if they boarded the boat. They would be terrified that what happened to their loved one would happen to them, and they would mentally replay the awful occurrence.

Overexcitement is a symptom that occurs when your nervous system is altered by a stressful incident, causing you to become hypersensitive. A loud noise or a bright light, for example, may cause anxiety. These are merely your natural survival instincts at work. You could also have difficulties sleeping or focusing. Such issues might make you bitter, turn off your happiness, and even wreck your life.

Symptoms of cognition and mood: the inability to recall the specific details of the traumatic incident is another evident indicator of PTSD. Some of the specifics may have been obscured by the adrenaline rush you were experiencing at the moment. You may then feel guilty or blame someone else for what occurred. You may experience a tremendous lot of guilt if you believe you had an opportunity to prevent the trauma but did not. Furthermore, PTSD might lead you to lose interest in previously enjoyed hobbies.

There are other approaches to treating post-traumatic stress disorder, but ACT is one of the most successful. It is, in fact, believed to be the most successful therapy method. In as few as twelve sessions, people with PTSD can be free of their symptoms.

The following are some of the techniques used to treat PTSD:

Long-Term Exposure

It's only normal for someone who has been through a terrible situation to avoid mental patterns that trigger those memories. This therapy strategy, on the other hand, tries to achieve precisely that: Over a long length of time, the person is exposed to the trauma's memories. This therapeutic strategy is based on the idea that if a person with PTSD confronts their anxieties, they would ultimately cease bothering them. If they continue to run away, however, the terrible memories will continue to have a significant influence on the individual. This therapy strategy has been lauded in multiple scientific studies for its efficiency in reducing repeated symptoms, anxiety arousal, and avoidance of PTSD-triggering situations. After only the third session, positive outcomes are possible.

Cognitive Processing Therapy is a type of cognitive processing therapy.

When a traumatic incident happens, the individual impacted may adopt a variety of maladaptive beliefs that serve to emphasize the severity of the experience. Cognitive processing therapy is used to help people discover and modify their thought habits. This strategy aids patients suffering from PTSD in making meaning of their experiences, reducing anxiety, and boosting self-esteem. Cognitive processing therapy has been demonstrated to be effective in the treatment of PTSD symptoms. The effectiveness of this therapy strategy is dependent in great part on the patient's cooperation.

In search of safety Your emotional fabric might be distorted when you go through a stressful incident. If you escape a road accident, for example, you will become extraordinarily sensitive. Something as innocuous as a bump in the road while driving may cause you to get worried, elicit a barrage of emotions, and take a long time to return to normal. People can overcome their emotional dysregulation and cope with their excessive anxiety by seeking protection. Mindfulness is one of the methods for resolving emotional dysregulation. It is less probable to return to the terrible past when your attention is focused on appreciating the current moment.

Desensitization of eye movement Reprocessing.

EMDR is comparable to extended exposure but employs eye movement exercises instead. This technique was popular a few years ago, but it appears to have lost favor among therapists once it was shown that eye movements have no effect. Some therapists, however, continue to employ this therapeutic strategy. The victim is asked to mentally relive their experience, and then the therapist takes them through different eye exercises, as is customary with extended exposure.

The efforts of PTSD sufferers to repress their thoughts have been demonstrated to be fruitless in studies. Unwanted thoughts, memories, and emotions become more frequent as a result of such techniques. Female PTSD patients who have been raped have demonstrated to have the biggest influence on this consequence.

Studies of self-reported coping mechanisms have also shown that avoidance tactics are effective.

Dissociation, which most likely happened during the original stress event, and delayed reactions have also been reported to aggravate PTSD symptoms.

ACT can be used to treat a wide range of illnesses, associated diseases, and daily life issues. It also covers a wide spectrum of reactions, not simply anxiety-based PTSD responses. Furthermore, ACT specifically tackles the issue of quality of life. A client can commit to behavior change and so enhance their quality of life via self-examination and awareness.

The ACT protocol is made up of three parts:

Creating Values Narratives - The client outlines his or her values and priorities in seven basic areas of life, including family, personal relationships, job, health, and spirituality, which is sometimes assigned as homework. With the therapist, these descriptions are examined and developed.

The customer begins by rating the value descriptors in absolute terms. Then he or she assesses how well they believe they have embodied these principles. Finally, they assign a score to each of these variables.

Identifying objectives, activities, and roadblocks - The client lists the items he or she wishes to accomplish. The steps that must be taken to attain these objectives have been highlighted. The customer then lists any potential roadblocks to these objectives. The therapist and the client then talk about ways to overcome certain challenges. Finally, the therapist works tirelessly to encourage the client to persevere in the face of adversity.

Chapter 5
Treating depression with Acceptance and Commitment therapy

Depression is defined as avoidance behavior and psychological immobility in the context of ACT. Depression is a collection of behaviors, thoughts, and feelings that are linked to a certain level of functioning. Depression-related activities are part of an effort to avoid personal experience.

Many persons with borderline personality disorder and similar mood and mental problems appear to lack the ability to cope with depression, which is a crucial skill. This does not, however, imply that all is lost. Many of your reactions are a result of a mix of learned behaviors and your surroundings. You can regain your capacity to withstand stress by relearning your strategies for processing and coping with emotions.

The ability to cope with stress, such as trauma, situations, and generally stressful occurrences, is emphasized heavily in ACT. In some circumstances, they are entirely unable to reason why certain things are occurring to them and why they are the way they are in a healthy way. Other types of treatment tend to concentrate on things like stating concerns or being proactive in dealing with them.

Because people who might benefit from ACT typically overcompensate when they try to assert difficulties in their life, ACT focuses on accepting things rather than actively altering them. In response to a certain stimuli, they may have an emotional overreaction or a variety of other issues. This is in contrast to the typical response to overwhelming stimuli, which is to become confused and perhaps stagnate until a clear path is provided.

As a result, ACT is given a lot of weight in order to guarantee that stressful stimuli do not cause you emotional anguish. To put it another way, don't let them bother you too much.

The capacity to cope with stressful situations is essential for living a happy and healthy life. If you don't have a regular, efficient, and healthy manner of coping with emotional trauma and general misery, you can't expect to be happy. There's a strong possibility you're taking this course because you're having trouble coping with your emotions when they arise.

You must understand that concealing or attempting to modify an out-of-control situation will frequently result in nothing, no matter how much you want it to. Things just happen from time to time. Accepting this is not a slacker attitude. It's a shirking mindset to refuse to accept it since it implies you're not up to the task at hand.

People frequently adopt a self-rejection attitude in reaction to external stimuli. When you try to modify or reject a circumstance, it shows you don't think you're capable of handling it. Thinking about what makes you feel this way and how to avoid these triggers is a part of Dialectical Behavior Therapy.

ACT includes a series of strategies that you may use to start practicing different approaches for building depression coping abilities. You should practice these techniques as often as possible in your regular life so that you can apply them instinctively when needed.

When you're stuck in a depression, go through them every day to keep them fresh in your memory. Also, try to keep them with you in some fashion so that you can remember what to do if you need to execute any of the activities listed.

Distraction techniques are the first type of activity that has been established. When an unpleasant sensation or scenario develops, you may utilize these to distract yourself and shift your focus away from it in a positive way. This will assist you in controlling your emotions. This works hand in hand with your mindfulness practice, because the capacity to focus that you learn through mindfulness helps you to rapidly transfer your attention elsewhere and cope with whatever is on your mind.

The accepts distraction approach is based on these concepts. It's a good idea to jot them all down on paper and then summarize them. Then, when you perform your depression block every morning after you wake up and every night before you go to bed, you may replenish them. This will assist you in developing a tolerance for unpleasant or stressful situations.

Another thing to concentrate on is finding a method to relax. Self-soothing is a notion that is particularly significant in Dialectical Behavior Therapy. Essentially, finding methods to be friendly and comforting to oneself is the goal.

We are not intended to run all the time without a stress-relieving method. You should take time to relax and enjoy the little things in life. These will assist you in decompressing and unloading. It's critical to take some time for yourself since it will help you refresh your thinking.

Staying in a high-stress situation and not allowing yourself to truly unwind and rest might exacerbate many people's emotional difficulties. While this will not fix all of your emotional difficulties at once, it will certainly assist you in working through them while traveling. Remembering that you have time to unwind later in the day might help you cope with the demands of the day. Take time for yourself and don't be scared to do it.

What should you do with yourself at this time? This is one of those instances where you have a genuine option. There is no such thing as a good or wrong way to act. It's all about being effective, much as the last guideline of meditation: do what's best for you!

There are a variety of things that might help you relax. Allow yourself time in the evening to take a bath, read literature from your preferred genre, or work on a hobby or project, for example. Just remember to be kind with yourself. Give yourself permission to unwind. Recognize that taking time for yourself is perfectly acceptable. This is a vital element of preventing depression, therefore include it in your daily routine.

To be honest, I'm going to stray for a bit. The truth is that the majority of persons who use ACT do so because they have borderline personality disorder. The outlook for those with borderline personality disorder is not good. Despite the fact that it is mostly curable with adequate counseling and potentially further depression medication, ten percent of persons with borderline personality disorder commit suicide. This is a terrible and terrifying character.

If you're reading this because you think you could have borderline personality disorder, or if you've read about it and think it might apply to you, I recommend seeing a doctor who can help you and talk you through your choices. Depression is real, it's serious, and it's frequently accompanied by borderline personality disorder. While anyone can benefit from the skills learned in Dialectical Behavior Therapy, if you're concerned that you might have Borderline Personality Disorder, you should seek professional help and enroll in a program with a personal therapist to ensure you get the best and most personalized experience possible.

The reason this is significant and not a pure digression is because maintaining the capacity to motivate oneself can be quite tough at times. If you suffer from depression as a result of a mood or personality problem, you probably have no idea what I'm talking about when I advise you should brighten up. While it's simple to suggest from a particular viewpoint that you should convince yourself that you can achieve anything, it's not true that you will believe it just because you tell yourself so.

You will probably not have an emotional reaction at first if you convince yourself that you can accomplish it, but you will ask yourself, "Can I do it?" "What if I'm not able to? What makes you think I'll be able to achieve it?" and that is a horrible beginning. Even if you don't believe it, you must imitate it until you succeed.

This is beneficial for a variety of reasons. Your brain eventually accepts what it is told, and if you tell it you can accomplish something, it will believe you can over time. What you say and do has a huge emotional impact. Faking success is a very real thing in terms of your brain structure, according to recent psychological studies.

Furthermore, telling yourself that you can do it, that you can accept anything and handle it appropriately, is tremendously powerful. It's a psychological weapon, to put it that way. If you do that, you will be able to take whatever life throws at you and work through it effectively. It's incredibly powerful to tell yourself that you can accomplish it.

Furthermore, you will gain the capacity to believe in yourself over time because you will know that you can achieve everything you set your mind to. Even if you don't believe it, you will always be able to do everything you set your mind to. Consider this: everything in life follows the same pattern. Either you advance or you reach rock bottom, and hitting rock bottom is death. You are still moving forward if you do not die. That information can provide you with peace of mind. Your mind is built to deal with a variety of situations, even if it isn't meant to deal with them right away. Your mind has a particularly difficult time with this since it is wired to deal with things in an unhealthy manner for one reason or another.

That does not rule out the possibility of reversing your decision. And, more crucially, the argument is that tough things are just difficult. You must work hard to overcome them, which is regrettably the nature of things. However, if you keep it in mind and struggle to embrace it, you will discover that when you tell yourself that you can overcome anything, you will eventually be able to do so. This will help you to feel more confident in your assertion.

The phrase also helps you to be more robust to whatever life throws at you. If you tell yourself often that you can manage anything, for example, you will remember yourself that you can handle anything if circumstances grow worse or something horrible happens. At the end of the day, you'll remember that you have the ability to make things happen. Your capacity to encourage and remind yourself that you can make it happen, whatever it takes, is your most powerful tool.

The specified enhancement set is now complete. As I previously stated, when performing the depression block, attempt to include these into your regular routine so that you can remember them when the time comes. Also, think about putting them where you can see them when you need them the most. This may be as simple as jotting them down in your phone's notes app and summarizing them so they're easy to find, or even taking a snapshot of the pages they're written on if you're using an app like Kindle or Books.

The ability to weigh the benefits and drawbacks of a situation is the second major feature of depression. Think about the position you're in and the benefits and drawbacks you could face if you choose not to endure it. Is there anything you can do to make a meaningful, proactive change?

When you deliberately strive not to do something, your mind frequently responds with a feedback reaction that persists until you act on it. (Unless you have OCD, of course.) This is most certainly a compulsion in such scenario, and you should avoid concentrating on it). You should evaluate a scenario realistically until you can adequately answer the question of what would happen if you reacted to it.

Overview

Module 1: Overview of Depression

Module 2: Thinking – Feeling Connection

Module 3: ACT

Module 4: Self-Compassion and Mindfulness

Module 5: Narrative Therapy – Story telling

Module 1: Overview of Depression

What is Depression?

Depression is a term used in plain English to express a variety of emotions such as sorrow, frustration, disappointment, and, at times, apathy.

Many people who are suffering from depressive symptoms may begin to question whether there is something really wrong with them. One common concern is that they are becoming insane. Unfortunately, other people's emotions and statements, such as "Don't act like a child!" are not particularly helpful.

Although you may feel alone in your battle against these emotions, the fact is that many people experience these moods frequently, if not on a daily basis. In fact, it is expected that one out of every four people will experience a seriously low mood at some point in their lives.

Depression may strike anyone at any age or stage of life. You may be an introvert or an extrovert, outgoing or reserved, young or old, male or female, rich or poor. You can get depressed regardless of your status. So keep in mind that you are not alone in this.

In psychology, the term "Depression" differs from the usual everyday feelings of symptoms in three main ways. Major depression is: 1) more intense, 2) lasts two weeks or more, and 3) it leads to inability to function normal in day to day tasks.

As a disorder, depression is a set of experiences and behaviors that characterize depressed people. You may find yourself experience all or part of these feelings and behaviors. The amount of symptoms and the level to which distinct symptoms are experienced vary greatly between individuals. These symptoms are discussed more below.

Mood

Depression is classified as a mood condition. Individuals who are depressed experience low mood that has lasted more than two weeks. Individuals suffering from moderate depression may not feel horrible all day, but they do experience a negative outlook and low mood. A great event may improve their mood, but even a slight disappointment might cause it to drop again. Low mood may remain throughout the day in severe depression, failing to rise even when pleasurable events occur. The mood may change during the day, being worse in the morning and somewhat better in the afternoon. This is known as 'diurnal variation,' and it is frequently associated with a more severe form of depression. In addition to low mood, the individual may experience feelings of inadequacy and worthlessness, guilt, anxiety and anger.

Cognitive symptoms

People with depression tend to see life in negative lenses. Individuals who are depressed have low self-esteem and low self-confidence. They constantly think about how bad they feel, how hopeless everything is and how bad life is.

Physical symptoms.

People with depression may experience problems with sleep. Some of the have difficulty falling asleep, others may wake during the night, or wake up early in the morning. Other may find difficulty staying awake.

The appetite changes and some people find themselves eating more than usual, while others eat less. Body weight changes as well.

People with depression have lower sexual interest.

They also have less energy and less motivation and may stop doing things they used to enjoy.

Module 2: Thinking – Feeling Connection

The Thinking-Feeling Connection

People frequently assume that their moods and emotions are influenced by the behavior of others, external events and the environment. "My partner made me so stressed," "My neighbor made me so upset," "The traffic lights made me feel so anxious," or "I'm feeling bad because I didn't get the job I wanted." We automatically assume that someone or something else is controlling our emotions.

We reach these conclusions without questioning whether or not the assumption is correct. However, if we learn how to stop analyzing we will find that there is a process in between.

How Do Our Thoughts Affect Our Feelings?

What truly causes us to feel and behave in the manner we do is frequently not the circumstance or another person's words or actions, but how we interpret that situation or that person's actions. How we perceive something or someone, as well as what we think about it or them, has a significant impact on how we feel. Our emotions and actions are heavily influenced by our ideas and beliefs about an event.

Here's an example. Suppose you went to a job interview. As you talk to your future employer, you notice that he does not look directly at you but often looks at the screen of his mobile phone. How would you feel if you though, "He is a very rude guy! " What if you thought, "I must be really failing in this. He seems not to like me. At this time, you probably realized that you felt different emotions as a result of the above mentioned thoughts. In reality, we do not have so much time to analyze our thoughts, because they are automatic and happen instantly. But, this is an example that our thoughts are there, and they affect the way we feel. Often, we find it difficult to find words for our feelings, so the words below can be a useful starting point in becoming able to understanding the connection between our thoughts and our feelings.

Words that describe feelings:

Angry Triggered   Tired Happy
      Excited   Joyful Annoyed
      Unhappy

Anxious Calm Scared   Sad   Cheerful
        Upset Nervous   Irritated   Bored

Automatic Thoughts

Just as we are not always conscious of the way we talk or walk, we are often not aware of our thoughts, which can vary from 70000 to 100000 every day. Our thinking, even automatic, helps us interpret the world around us, explaining us what is happening, interpreting events, sounds, smells, feelings and much more. Thoughts come and go all the time, especially automatic thoughts, that play important role in our well-being.

There are three kinds of automatic thoughts:

Neutral thoughts, For example: "I think I will go to the bank today"

Positive thoughts, For example: "I like dancing, I am so skilled at it".

Negative thoughts, For example: "I cannot complete this task, I must be stupid.

How Do Our Thoughts Affect Our Feelings?

Automatic thoughts frequently represent fears and anxieties, but they may also be about anything we have ever seen, heard, or learned. Furthermore, it might be anything we know about from any source. Negative automatic thoughts, on the other hand, are clearly the ones that might give us emotional pain. People who are depressed have bad views about themselves, the world around them, and their future, and it is these negative beliefs that may be modified to help you overcome your depression

Cognitive behavioral therapy says that following after an event, we give meaning to it through our thoughts and then we starting to feel the way we feel.

EVENT ⟹ Meaning we give to the event ⟹ Feelings

These thoughts result in our physical and emotional reactions.

Event	Thoughts	Emotion	Behavior
Hit a bicyclist with the car	I will go to jail	fear	Driving away with the car
My boss treats my unfairly	He must hate me	Anger, frustration	Defensive, disobedient

Automatic words...

- ❖ Can be thoughts, memories, sound, words that we tend to automatically believe that they are valid.

- ❖ Can happen at any time, as they are automatic.

- ❖ Are ours and they represent our experiences, values, culture, and knowledge.

- ❖ Are habitual and persistent and do not go away. They repeat over and over again and the more resistant we put, the more persistent they get.

Feelings are not Thoughts

When we initially try to distinguish between ideas and feelings, it is easy to get them mixed up. We may be accustomed to discussing thoughts and feelings as if they were two sides of the same coin, but it is more beneficial to separate them and remember that feelings are not thoughts.

Try the exercise on the following page and see if you can distinguish the feelings and thoughts in each of the scenarios.

Exercise: Distinguish thoughts from feelings

Read the following scenarios and identify the feelings that may result from the thoughts.

Scenario A

You have had a tiring day at work and you just arrived home to find dishes dirty in the sink, the faucet running and your partner sitting in front of the television playing video games.

1) You think

"What a nightmare. I have had a long day and now I come home to this! Life is unfair! He doesn't care about me, only about himself!."

Possible feelings:

____

____

2) You think

''I must have done something to deserve this. I am a bad partner. I don't deserve him. He is right to ignore me.''

Possible feelings:

____

____

Scenario B

One day your boss asks you to go over to their office for a meeting. As you arrive, you noticed that the door is closed. You knock and no one comes to answer. You turn the doorknob, open the door and you find your boss and all your colleagues standing in front of you shouting ''Surprise'' and continue to sing ''Happy Birthday''.

1) You think

''Wow'' What a nice surprise. I wasn't expecting this''

Possible feelings:

____

____

2) You think

''Everybody must like me''

____

____

The ABC Analysis

We've discussed how our thoughts influence how we feel. If we are joyful and thrilled, we have most likely been having positive thoughts and thinking about wonderful things. On the other side, if we are nervous, depressed, or disturbed, we have most certainly been having negative thoughts (these are referred to be harmful thoughts, because they lead in unpleasant feelings or unproductive behaviors). We all have moments when we consider things that make us sad or nervous, and this is a natural part of life. However, if you frequently feel worried or nervous, you may need to evaluate your thoughts in order to enhance your mood.

If these automatics thoughts lead to uncomfortable feelings, it may be logical to conclude that the most effective thing to do is to change those unhelpful thoughts to helpful ones. So, how do you go about doing that? To begin changing the way you feel, you must first learn to recognize when problematic automatic thoughts come and then try to replace them using the ABC analysis.

ABC Analysis.

As mentioned above every behavior and thoughts is activated by an event. In the ABC analysis, we start to determine this Activating Event (A), by writing down the situation or the setting in which we had these uncomfortable feelings, such as depression. Write down the scene in details, the way a camera would do. Just state the facts without explaining or describing any thoughts.

The following stage is to determine the 'C,' which stands for 'Consequences,' which comprises both your emotions and your behavior/action. Make a list of the words that best describe your emotions. Underline the word that best describes the emotion you were experiencing at the moment. Then, on a scale of 0 to 100, assess the intensity of this emotion. The greater the number, the stronger the reaction. You should also make a note of any behaviors that you carried out, for example, closing the all the doors and going to bed.

Now, remembering the circumstances and your emotions, find the 'B,' which symbolizes your 'Beliefs,' or thoughts, expectations, perceptions, and attitudes. For example: "What was I thinking about at the time the telephone started to ring?" "What thoughts were going through my mind?" Make a list of all of your thoughts. When you've finished this, go through each thought and highlight the one that is most linked with the predominant feeling you had during the 'A.' We'll now refer to it as your hot thought. Now, on a scale of 0 to 100, rate how strongly you believe this though. Let's look at an example. Imagine walking into your boss's office feeling anxious. To do an ABC analysis, you might ask yourself, "How am I making myself anxious? What am I thinking?" You might identify a thought such as, "I don't want to be here." If you only had this thought, you'd probably not experience a strong emotion but only feel mildly anxious. If you do experience a strong emotional response to this thought, it probably indicates that there are other thoughts underlying this thought. Therefore, the thought, "I don't want to be here" is only an initial thought, and you would need to discover what other unhelpful thoughts were present to invoke such a strong emotional response. For example: ''Maybe he is going to fire me''.

Exercise: ABC Record and thought diary

Your goal should be to become an expert at spotting your unhelpful thoughts.

A Activating Event	B Believable Thoughts	C Consequences	
What, where, when, external event or internal trigger (real or imagined) For example: I got caught cheating in exams.	What did I think at that time? For example: I thought that they will terminate my studies.	Consequences of believing the thought For example: I started feeling anxious and I was breathing fast, therefore I panicked and ran out of the examinations room.	Consequences of not believing the thought For example: I understood what I did was wrong, so I apologized and I moved on.

Module 3: ACT

Acceptance and Commitment Therapy

Acceptance and Commitment Therapy, or ACT, is a type of Cognitive Behavioral Therapy that is best described as a process in which people confront and modify their understanding of their past experiences. This means that when an individual has experienced something traumatic that affects them for the rest of their life, and impacts their relationships and other aspects of their life, ACT will take over, giving a new meaning to that event, helping them become resilient and more psychologically flexible. ACT helps the individual to take control of their life.

Who will benefit?

ACT will be beneficial to individuals who experienced traumatic events, tragedies, hurt and loss and to those who want to gain control of their lives. ACT will give them meaning to their experiences and allow them to change their pain into motivation for something greater and better.

How to use ACT

ACT is a great process of self-expression and a helpful tool in finding what is important to you. It is also great because it helps you clarify your values and emphasizes action to increase wellbeing, as opposed to keeping an apathetic stance because of your negative thoughts.

Worksheets.

1. Values Bullseye

The values bullseye exercise helps you reflect and put your feelings into words, while also help you understand what is important. It also helps you to identify your values and how you want to live your life.

Step 1: Identifying our values

The bullseye exercise begins similarly to other standard value-finding exercises. Your first step is to identify your values and what is most important to you in life. What are you primary thoughts, feelings and actions that affect your life? After you identify your values, you will categorize them into four main categories: 1) leisure, 2) relationships, 3) personal growth and health, and 4) work and education.

1.Leisure refers to how you enjoy yourself, how you have fun ore relax; recreation, your hobbies, activities for fun or rest. For example: adventure, connection with others, experiences..

____

____

2. Relationships refers to intimacy, friendships and connections with others. This category includes relationships with your parents, partners, children, relatives, friends, colleagues and other social relationships. What kind of relationships do you want? How do you want to be in these relationships?

For example: love, intimacy, respect, connection with others..

____

____

3. Personal growth and health refers to your personal development, physical and mental health, spiritual development and others. For example: health, physical appearance, exercise...

____

____

4. Work and education refers to your education, career, knowledge and development. What personal qualities do you want to possess? What skills do you want to develop? For example: accomplishment, aspiration, justice..

____

____

You have probably noticed that some values fall in more than one category. This is perfectly normal. You will also notice later that the same values may not show up in the same spot on the bullseye. Note that values are not goals and the easier way to distinguish, is to understand that goal are something you want to do, while values is how you want to live your life.

Step2: Recognizing how close we are to living our values

After you've written down your values for each category, mark an X on the bullseye according on how close you're living your values on a daily basis. The centre of the bullseye indicates that this value is something that guides your thoughts and activities on a daily basis. The outermost ring, on the other hand, indicates that you aren't living by your ideals and that they aren't as important to you. Consider why you have placed your values on that particular ring. Can you think of any examples of this value being demonstrated in your life? What would it look like to live totally in accordance with your values?

Take "connection with others" as an example. You may put this in the centre of the bullseye and in the leisure ring, but on the outside of the relationships ring. This would suggest that when you are having leisure time, you connect with others, but when you are in a relationship, you might not pay much attention to your connection with the other person. You can place an X on the bullseye for the values that are lacking attention and start to spend some time thinking about why you're doing so.

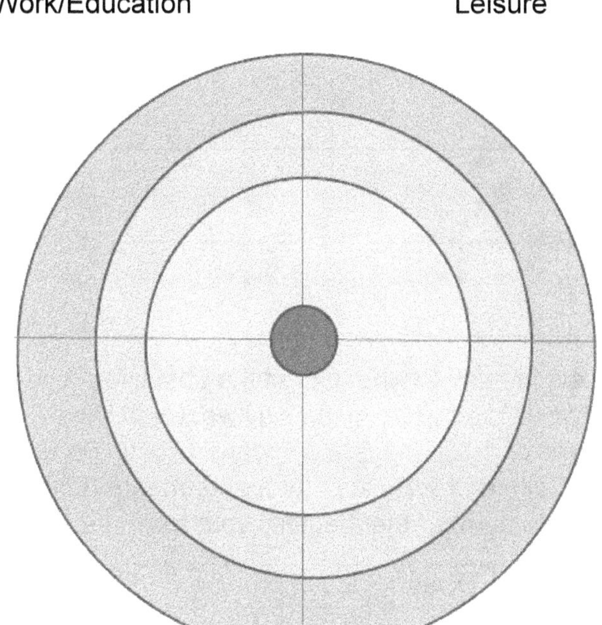

Step 3: Identify obstacles that interfere with living our values

1) Now, based on what we have written in our areas of value, we now need to write down the obstacles that interfere with living our life as we want to. What stands between us and living our life as we would like to? For example: for intimacy the obstacle could include the fear getting hurt emotionally or the fear of getting rejected. For building a more intimate

relationship obstacles could include: working a lot of hours, neglecting my partner and so on.

Obstacle 1:

____

Obstacle 2:

____

Obstacle 3:

____

2) Lets identify to what extent the obstacle prevents us from living our life in the way we would like to. On a scale of 1 to 7, where 1 means "doesn't prevent me at all" and 7 means "prevents me completely" mark the number that best fits your estimate.

Obstacle	Doesn't prevent me at all (1)	2	3	4	5	6	Prevents me completely (7)
1							
2							
3							

Step 4: Create an action plan

With your bullseye in hand, it's time to draw a strategy for completely living your values and in turn, to push those Xs closer to the centre. Perhaps you need to develop healthier habits around something essential to you. Or maybe you could spend less time toxic relationships. Identifying the obstacles that prevent you from living your values can provide you with an action plan. Is there anything more you should be doing? Or is it something you should do less?

Now, try to identify at least one action you are willing to take towards bringing each values closer to the centre.

1.Leisure. For example: to have more fun the action could be to work less hours and spend more time with myself, or looking for more adventures..

____

____

2. Relationships. For example: to build an intimate relationship the action could be to focus on my wellbeing and my emotions, pay more attention to my partner, be more expressive..

____

____

3. Personal growth and health. For example: If I want to improve my communication skills then I could take specialized courses, or seek therapy..

____

____

4. Work and education. For example: if I want a career, then I could focus in improving my skills and knowledge in my field of work..

____

____

Module 4: Self-Compassion and Mindfulness

Compassion for oneself is fundamentally the same as compassion for others. Consider what it's like to feel compassion. To feel compassion for others, you must first recognize that they are in pain. If you ignore the homeless person on the street, you will be unable to feel compassion for him and his experience. Also, having compassions means to feel the pain of others, to suffer with them. When this happens, you experience a sense of warmth, care, and immediately you want to help that person in any way. Compassion, makes you realize that we are not perfect and that we all can suffer and fail.

Self-compassion entails treating oneself the same way when you are having a tough time, failing, or noticing anything you don't like about yourself. Instead of just rejecting yourself, you pause and ask yourself, "This is extremely painful right now," ''How can I soothe myself in this moment? Self-compassion implies you are compassionate and understanding when confronted with personal faults rather than relentlessly criticizing and blaming oneself for different deficiencies or weaknesses.

The three elements of Self-compassion:

1. Self-kindness

Self-compassion means being warm and sympathetic toward ourselves when we struggle, fail, or feel inadequate, rather than dismissing our sorrow or shaming ourselves. Self-compassionate individuals understand that being flawed, failing, and going through life issues is unavoidable, thus they prefer to be kind with themselves when presented with painful situations rather than being upset when life falls short of predetermined expectations.

2. Humanity

Frustration at not getting what we desire is frequently accompanied by an unreasonable sense of isolation - as if "I" am the only one who is suffering. However, all humans suffer. Self-compassion entails acknowledging that suffering and personal inadequacy are part of the common human experience – something that we all go through rather than something that only "me" goes through.

3. Mindfulness

Self-compassion also necessitates a balanced attitude to our unpleasant emotions, so that they are not suppressed or exaggerated. This results from the process of linking our experiences to those of others who are also suffering. It also comes from being willing to notice our unpleasant thoughts and feelings with openness and clarity, so that they may be retained in conscious awareness. Mindfulness is a non-judgmental state of mind in which one observes thoughts and feelings as they are, without trying to conceal or reject them. Mindfulness helps you tune in to the present moment.

There are many ways to practice mindfulness. Some examples include:

Pay attention: Try to intentionally bring an accepting attention to everything you do. Find joy in simple pleasures. For example: Smelling the roses.

Accept yourself: Try to treat yourself the way you would treat a friend. For example: I failed in physics, but is it okay. I will succeed the next time.

Focus on your breathing: For example: When your thoughts are running, try to sit down and take a deep breath. Close your eyes and focus on your breath as it moves

in and out of your body.

Meditation: Medication can be done in two ways: (1) sitting, (2)walking

1) Sit comfortably with your back straight, feet flat on the floor and hands in your lap. Inhale through your nose, exhale from your mouth. Notice how your breath moves your body. If your thoughts interrupt your meditation, return your attention to your breath.

2) Find a quiet place, and begin to walk slowly. Focus on your walk, being aware of the physical sensations. When you reach the end of your path,

turn and continue walking, keeping attention to the sensations.

Mindfulness = Gratitude

Everyone can benefit from making an effort to practice mindfulness every day. Mindfulness can help you become more grateful and appreciative of the good things in your life. Therefore, it is important to start to notice and identify the things you are grateful for. Be mindful of the small details in your daily life and notice how many good things you take for granted.

Expressing gratitude is more than being polite. It is about showing your true heartfelt feelings. For example, when we want to thank someone, we usually say "thank you". This time, instead, we should notice something good on them and genuinely appreciate it.

Exercise:

- Show your appreciation to someone who did something nice. For example: A stranger carried your groceries to the car. Say: "It was really king of you to help me", or "Thank you for your kind deed".

- Express gratitude by paying it forward. For example: A stranger carried your groceries to the car and you "Held the door open for a stranger behind you".

- Tell people how you feel and what they mean to you. For example: "Dad, thanks for raising me up the way you did", "Mom, delicious dinner, Thank you".

Module 5: Narrative Therapy – Story telling

Narrative therapy or Story telling is a part of ACT that allows you the become aware of your strengths and values. It can also help you to identify your skills which can help you deal with daily life's problems.

How Narrative Therapy – Story telling works

Writing about your problems can help you to get an insight of your strengths, values, emotions and goals which in turn can help you to come up with effective solutions. After writing down your life story, you will be asked to complete a worksheet containing two exercises with questions. Answer the questions according to each exercise, by providing as much detail as possible.

Life Story

The Past, Present the Future

Writing a story about your life can help you bring attention to your experience and your values. It will help you put your thoughts into words and use them to act on them. You are expected to gain a greater sense of meaning, which can contribute to your happiness.

The Past

Write a story about your past and include any challenges you have experience, how you overcame them and what strengths or skill allowed you to do so.

____

____

The Present

Write a story about your present and describe you life and who you are at this moment. How are you different from your past self? What challenges are you facing now? What are your strengths?

____

____

The Future

Write about your ideal future. How would you want you life to be 10 years from now? How will you be different from the person you are now?

____

____

Worksheet – Answer the Questions:

Exercise 1

Write in detail about a traumatic event/situation that you faced recently

____

____

How did you respond?

____

____

What is your biggest strength?

____

____

How could you use this strength to deal with the traumatic event?

____

____

Exercise 2

Write in detail about an event in which you felt rejected or disappointed

____

____

How did you respond?

____

____

How did you cope up with the event?

____

____

How would you handle it differently using your skills?

____

Summary

- ❖ Depression is caused by the combination of biological and psychological factors.

- ❖ Depression symptoms may include low mood, low energy, lack of motivation, a tendency to think negative, guilt, anxiety, anger and feelings of inadequacy and worthlessness.

- ❖ What drives us to feel the way we do is not other people or situations, rather our own thoughts and beliefs in response to those.

- ❖ There are 3 kinds of thoughts: neutral, positive, and negative

- ❖ If we feel negative, it is often because we are thinking negative.

❖ If we want to improve how we feel, we need to become aware of what we think and change our thoughts.

Consistent and continuous practice of the strategies you learned will help you to integrate them into your lifestyle.

Chapter 6
Beat anxiety with Acceptance and Commitment therapy

People who suffer from anxiety must deal with unwelcome ideas that spring into their brains. Your intrusive thoughts are sometimes caused by the nature of your worry. Persons with generalized anxiety, for example, are more likely to have intrusive thoughts about one of their loved ones, whereas people with social phobias are more likely to have intrusive thoughts about a time when they humiliated themselves. Anxiety can take many forms, including:

Generalized Anxiety Disorder (GAD) is:

Anxiety about social situations

Agoraphobia

Selective mutism is a kind of selective mutism that occurs when

Separation Panic disorder is a kind of anxiety condition.

Phobias with a specific focus

In any given year, about 12% of the population suffers from an anxiety illness. Anxiety disorders affect between 5% and 30% of people at some time in their life. Between the ages of 15 and 35, it is most common. A phobia is the most frequent kind of anxiety condition. Anxiety disorders can be caused by both hereditary and environmental factors. It can be triggered by past trauma, such as child maltreatment or adversity (e.g., poverty). Anxiety disorders can occur in conjunction with other mental illnesses such as depression and personality disorders. Anxiety disorders, or a combination of problems, can impose such a burden on the body that it can lead to heart disease, substance misuse, or hyperthyroidism. Anxiety disorders are commonly treated with cognitive behavioral therapy and pharmacological medications. Self-help tools are popular among OCD sufferers, and mindfulness exercises are beneficial.

What causes you to be worried?

Anxiety is merely a fear that you have about the future. Anxiety disorders will have a significant impact on your quality of life. You get into the habit of perceiving issues where none exist. Anxiety gives your life an intense character, forcing you to retreat and isolate or become angry. Both extremes have a tendency to suffocate social cohesiveness.

What are the symptoms of anxiety?

When you're nervous or afraid, your body and mind are both functioning too quickly. Some of the things that can happen as a result of worry and dread are listed below:

Heart rate has increased.

Breathing rate has increased

Muscle weakness

Sweating profusely

Lack of concentration due to stomach pain

Dizziness

The sensation of being frozen

Appetite loss.

Sweats that are both hot and chilly

Muscle tenseness

Mouth is dry

Anxiety's physical symptoms can be aggravating, especially if you don't know what's generating your dread or anxiety. There are various anxiety triggers, and the brain occasionally sends these messages needlessly. Strengthening your self-awareness is the only way to increase your ability to comprehend your anxiety relationship.

Anxiety Attacks

This is a situation in which you are overcome by anxiety-related mental and bodily symptoms. Sufferers describe trouble breathing, a racing heart, and the bizarre sensation of losing their minds.

Worry

This is the exaggeration of difficulties to the point that a person believes the future is dark. Worriers have little hope and believe that bad things will happen at some point in the future.

The following are some ways for overcoming fear, worry, anxiety, sadness, and pretty much any other mental disorder:

Confront your worries.

It may seem paradoxical, but it is the best course of action. When you address your worries instead of avoiding them, you earn more strength. You get something precious when you face your fears: knowledge. This is how you disprove myths and find practical solutions to your anxieties.

Know who you are.

To overcome your anxieties in a healthy way, you must first have a better awareness of who you are. What is the source of your apprehensions? What was it like growing up for you? Because we know that our early upbringing and experiences molded the majority of our views and concerns, it's critical to learn everything you can about yourself.

Workout

A exercise needs your undivided focus. Your mind will be diverted from its anxieties and concentrated on the work at hand in this manner. This is a fantastic method for overcoming your worries and concerns. Exercise also improves heart health, which leads to better blood circulation and a stronger immune system, which successfully reduces negative emotions.

Relax

Your fears are displaced when you relax your body and thoughts. Deep breathing might help you attain this level of tranquility. To do so, sit in a meditation position and breathe in and out while clearing your mind of distractions. This assists in restoring equilibrium to the body.

Consume nutritious foods.

A balanced diet is essential for mental and emotional well-being. A healthy diet emphasizes essential nutrients while avoiding junk food. You want to keep your blood sugar levels in check. Panic attacks and anxiety are more likely when your blood sugar levels decrease.

Alcohol should be used in moderation or avoided entirely.

It's tempting to drink a couple bottles when you're scared. However, keep in mind that the happiness that follows is just temporary. You can't drink your way to happiness. Rather, learn to confront your worries and anxieties when sober. This is far more productive.

Faith

It's useful to trust that if you believe in a supernatural presence looking over the universe and the people who live in it, it will aid you. The more you think this supernatural creature will reach out to you, the more likely it is that you will be able to overcome your worries and concerns.

Medication

Medicines are useful for persons who are short on time. They may not be the greatest treatment strategy, but when used in conjunction with other approaches, medicines may be quite beneficial.

Groups that provide assistance

There are many people who, like you, deal with concerns and anxieties. You don't even have to look hard to locate these folks thanks to the internet. Forums, Facebook groups, websites, and so forth are all available. However, before you join a support group, you should learn about its guiding principles to see whether you are a good fit.

Chapter 7
Manage aggression with ACT

Gripping, shoving, and slapping are the most prevalent forms of physical hostility, although more serious violence is less common (including forcible restraint and hitting). Despite the fact that males are more likely to perform significant aggressive actions, such as dominating women, research reveals that both men and women engage in the most prevalent kinds of violent behavior.

Aggression and its causes have been better understood thanks to extensive study, but treatment choices are limited. The majority of therapy approaches are old and lack scientific basis. In contextual behavioral science, risk variables have been employed to develop a model. Psychological and physical aggressiveness are considered as ways to escape or avoid unpleasant personal experiences in this approach. The unique approach investigates the processes that drive therapy and integrates connected strategies and components of treatment.

Depression, anxiety, drug abuse, and health disorders, as well as marital issues, separation, and divorce, are all linked to physical aggressiveness. Aggression, in general, exacerbates problems like depression and relationship management. It has a negative impact on both occupational and cognitive performance.

Aggression is linked to the following risk factors:

1. family - partner aggression in non-aggressive adult relationships is discussed in families with rigorous discipline, limited cohesiveness, and intense disputes.

2. Relationship - Aggression is associated with relationship breakdown and disruption, which is exacerbated by interpersonal skills deficiencies that increase the likelihood of conflict within the pair.

3. Personality and psychopathy - the most important indicators are personality and psychopathy, which are likely based in childhood or teenage antisocial behavior, childhood trauma or abuse, depression, and conduct disorder. Partner aggressiveness is linked to pathologies of the II axis (e.g., antisocial personality disorder and borderline personality disorder), which can be worsened by depression and maladaptive attachment patterns linked to anxiety, unstable self-esteem, and impulsivity.

4. Cognitive and emotional aspects - the most researched factor is anger. The issue might be related to how people react to rage. Fear, guilt, and envy, as well as symptoms experienced by panic attack sufferers, may all play a role. There is some shaky evidence based on aggressive people's self-reports that suggests cognitive biases and illogical beliefs, as well as victim blaming, may play a role.

5. other variables - drug misuse, stress, and relationship qualities are all being investigated, but it's unclear how these elements influence aggressiveness. Arguments and verbal aggressiveness frequently accompany

psychological and physical violence, implying that such verbal squabbles may serve as a precursor to other forms of hostility.

INTERNAL EXPERIENCE > AGGRESSION > RELIEF > STIMULUS (interpersonal conflict)

ACT's purpose is to change the emotional reaction. Aggressive conduct can be minimized by lessening the urge to control one's innermost feelings. The person acknowledges and articulates the aggressive strategy's impact, as well as his or her own avoidance and control methods. The therapist teaches more adaptive answers so that the client can unlearn the old strategy's stringent avoidance principles. The therapist guides the person's actions toward values-based objectives. In order to proceed in a new path, the individual discusses and investigates his or her fundamental values. In the group of people who participate in relationship violence, working on values is critical.

Chapter 8
How to stop intrusive and Obsessive thoughts

Obsessive-compulsive disorder (OCD) is characterized by a severe type of intrusive thinking. They induce the patient to have a negative attitude about their thoughts. In essence, the individual believes there is something wrong with them since they are plagued with intrusive thoughts. Intrusive thoughts cause obsessive-compulsive disorder sufferers a great deal of anguish, and their attempts to eliminate these thoughts lead to a worsening of their condition.

Cognitive behavioral therapies (CBT), of which ACT is one, are the most widely prescribed treatments for OCD. The basic symptoms of OCD, according to the Medline Plus Medical Dictionary, are unwelcome obsessive thoughts, sensations, feelings, ideas, and actions. For persons with obsessive-compulsive disorder, sensations are obsessions.

It's entirely natural to check to see if your door is secured from time to time. If you have an obsessive-compulsive personality, on the other hand, you will constantly check to verify if the door is truly locked. Obsessive thoughts and compulsive behaviors may easily overwhelm a person, causing them to deviate from their usual routine. In the face of these ideas, the person feels powerless.

Obsessive-compulsive disorder (OCD) is characterized by uncontrolled thoughts and compulsion to undertake ritualized, recurrent actions. OCD patients feel their thoughts and behaviors are nonsensical, yet they are unable to break free from their repetitive patterns.

The following are the different types of persons who have obsessive-compulsive disorder:

Launderers are concerned about infecting microorganisms. They feel compelled to clean.

Checkers are continually on the lookout for objects that might cause injury or danger.

Doubters and sinners are worried that if everything isn't done correctly, something bad will happen.

Counters and arrangers are obnoxious about symmetry and order.

Hoarders are people who are scared to throw away whatever they own for fear of anything bad happening.

Regardless matter how obsessive your disorder's symptoms appear, there are a variety of strategies to help you overcome it. The first step is to stop doing the things that make your obsessions worse.

Do not run away from your anxieties.

Avoiding your worries may appear to be a wise decision, but the more you avoid them, the more you encourage the recurrence of your obsessions and exacerbate your anxiety. You must learn to accept your triggers for as long as possible if you wish to be free of them. Allow yourself to be exposed to your OCD triggers and then resist the impulse to do a routine. If you are not psychologically prepared, this might be fairly difficult, but you can vary the intensity of your ritual. The more you expose yourself to your OCD triggers, the less anxiety you'll experience and the faster you'll be able to manage your thoughts.

Prepare for obsessive habits.

Recognize and address the events that cause your OCD to flare up. For example, if you have a habit of checking to verify if doors are secured, do not shut the door carelessly and walk away the next time. Carefully close the door and double-check that it is securely shut. Do not be hurried. When you leave, you'll feel less compelled to double-check the door since you'll know you double-checked it. Use your imagination to conjure up a vivid image of a closed door or drawn curtains, and label it "The door is locked." You may just bring the image to mind whenever you feel compelled to check on the door or curtains, and correctly classify that thinking as a "compulsive thought."

Redirect your concentration.

When you have an obsessive idea, don't dwell on it; instead, concentrate on anything else. Exercise, go for a jog, read a book, watch a movie, meet up with a buddy, or listen to music are all options. The objective is to introduce a fresh train of thinking to replace your compulsion. You effectively delay your reaction to the obsessive idea by diverting your attention for at least fifteen minutes. When you redirect your mind to anything else, you will notice that the need diminishes or fades entirely.

Make a list of your obsessive ideas.

From time to time, everyone has troublesome ideas. People with obsessive-compulsive disorder, on the other hand, are trapped in a whirlpool of obsessive thoughts. These thoughts repeat themselves in their heads until they succumb to the pattern. As ideas come to mind, jot them down. Write down every obsessive idea that comes to mind with a pen and paper or your favorite device.

Make a concern time for those with OCD.

Rather than fighting your urges and impulses, simply put them off. You might have two concern periods during the day. However, you should schedule these sessions when you are not experiencing anxiety. If you have obsessive thoughts outside of the worry session, write them down so you can think about them during the worry period.

Keep a journal of your obsessive ideas.

Keep a journal of your obsessive ideas. Concentrate on one fixation at a time and capture it on your gadget. Make sure you take detailed notes on the sort of fixation you're dealing with. Then, again and over, watch or listen to yourself describe your obsessive ideas. You will be less influenced by your anxieties and obsessions if you tackle them on a regular basis.

Nicotine and alcohol should be avoided.

Although alcohol lessens tension and concern, the impact is only temporary. When the affects of alcohol wear off, anxiety increases dramatically. Cigarettes also make you feel anxious. When you indulge in these vices, you fall into a never-ending loop of negative thoughts. It is preferable to confront your OCD when sober.

Increase the amount of time you spend with your friends and family.

Obsessive thoughts may make your life so difficult that you feel alone. However, do not allow it to reach that stage. When you're alone, the affects of OCD become more obvious. To feel more grounded, spend time with your loved ones.

Chapter 9
ACT vs DBT

ACT is a type of psychotherapy that emphasizes experiences, self-awareness, and value orientation. Dialectical Behavior Therapy (DBT) is a type of cognitive behavioral therapy that emphasizes teamwork, patient support, and the development of skills to deal with difficult emotional circumstances. Originally designed to help patients who were having suicidal thoughts, this medication is now used to treat a wide range of additional disorders linked to poor emotion management.

Dialectical behavior treatment is divided into two categories:

Weekly individual counseling sessions

Group treatment sessions are held once a week.

The following are some of the most important DBT skills and practices to master: Skills in Objectivity and Effectiveness

Describe: Your capacity to grasp your inner sensations is explained by this. The patient must find the appropriate words to express their feelings. DBT allows the patient to become aware of their genuine feelings. The more a patient can describe their problem, the more likely they are to receive assistance.

A patient should be able to articulate his or her needs and desires. If he has a suggestion on how to better his circumstances, he should share it with others and make the most of the resources available to him.

Assertion: DBT treatment encourages patients to take control of their lives rather than feeling helpless victims. Their aggressiveness demonstrates their dominance. Being assertive does not entail being confrontational or arrogant; rather, it is a method of expressing one's demands and standing firm in one's beliefs.

Reinforce yourself: no matter how good your ideas or goals are, you'll always need some kind of support to see them through. As a result, a patient should tackle every difficulty with the understanding that they will need to reinforce their thoughts before achieving their goals.

Mindful: This ability allows the patient to return their attention to the present moment. A patient should learn to focus with a laser beam rather than allowing his thoughts roam and ponder about the numerous things he is concerned with or disengaged from. This is a critical component in the battle against mental health issues.

Self-assurance: It is critical to have a high level of self-assurance. Although self-confidence does not allow you to move mountains, it does provide you with an optimistic outlook, which is a significant advantage. The more self-assurance you have, the more likely you are to attract positive situations and achieve advancement in your life.

DBT enables a patient to understand their own power. They have the ability to question the present order or the way things are done. As a result, a patient should strive to negotiate terms and seek out options that are beneficial to him. If he succeeds in establishing new terms by using his negotiating power, his self-esteem will rise.

Relationship abilities

DBT encourages patients to treat their partners with kindness. If they use a delicate approach, their partner will be more receptive to them. However, if they are tough with their spouse and do not pay attention to how they treat them, there will be a lot of issues.

DBT stresses displaying interest rather than hope that your spouse recognizes how much you respect them. Partners are extremely sensitive to the small things that are done or not done, and this may make all the difference in a relationship's success or failure.

Validate: The notion that we don't require validation is erroneous. The fact is that we require affirmation from those who are important to us. Our relationship partners are significant enough, and we value their approval. But, just as you desire affirmation from your partner, you must reciprocate so that the relationship does not become poisonous.

Effectiveness - Skills - Self-Esteem

Fairness: You must always endeavor to be fair. This means that you must be fair to others, but even more crucially, to yourself. Allowing people to have their way at your expense is never a good idea. No one else will take care of you if you do not take care of yourself. Being truthful is a positive start in the right path.

Please accept my apologies: you will have unpleasant interactions with others. If you've done anything wrong, you should apologize, and if you've done something wrong, you should want an apology. Although a requested apology isn't ideal, it does demonstrate that the attacker has genuine intentions.

Truthful: The one thing you owe yourself and the world is to tell the truth. Although it isn't extremely prevalent, it can't harm. It also makes your life easier.

Increased psychological flexibility and a greater focus on the present are the goals of Acceptance and Commitment Therapy (ACT).

The following are some of the ACT principles:

Acceptance Everyone has a problem with negative thinking. They strive to conceal these ideas instinctively, but is it worth it? Patients are taught to tolerate their negative ideas using ACT. They must create space for negative emotions, impulses, and experiences. The seeming abundance mindset makes it simpler to let go of the bad things that have always piqued your curiosity.

Distraction of the mind

This means you have an autonomous perception of your ideas, words, images, and other cognitive activity. They should stand for just what they say and not be merged into a wider concept. This is the polar opposite of cognitive fusion, which involves attempting to "fuse" several cognitions into a single mental output. The words "chocolate cake," for example, are enough to make us salivate since they conjure up a mental image of a cake. They can utilize cognitive defusion to avoid attaching a lot of significance to the images and words that come to mind.

DBT is a kind of cognitive behavioral therapy.

Clients and therapists have a continuous interaction in DBT. Clients are encouraged to collaborate with their therapists to tackle their life problems in this style of treatment. Individuals must role-play new ways of interacting with people, complete homework assignments, and practice skills like self-soothing when disturbed in order to achieve this.

These abilities are given to patients in weekly lectures and homework groups, and they are an important aspect of DBT. Individual therapists can assist their clients acquire DBT skills and apply them to their lives in this way.

DBT has four phases.

DBT treatment is generally broken down into four parts. The severity of a client's conduct is used to place them to one of these levels. To assist their clients, therapists are urged to follow the framework described in these steps. These levels do not have a set time limit. Depending on the client's purpose, the therapist and client can take as much time as they need.

The first stage

The client is typically sick and has lost control at this point, and they may attempt self-harm, use drugs, or participate in other self-destructive behaviors. When such clients begin DBT, they may describe their situation as "hell."

This phase's major purpose is to assist the client in transitioning from a state of being out of control to one in which he learns to be more in charge of himself.

The second stage

Clients in stage two frequently feel hopeless about their life. They may have control over their destructive actions, yet they continue to suffer as a result of devaluation or prior trauma. This frequently causes their emotional experience to be disrupted.

The major purpose of the second stage is to assist these individuals in overcoming their despair and reclaiming their emotional experiences. This stage includes the treatment of patients with post-traumatic stress disorder (PTSD).

The third level

The purpose at this level is to encourage patients to live, discover pleasure and tranquility, and improve their self-esteem. The therapist assists the client in leading a regular life that includes both joyful and sad times.

The fourth and final stage

A fourth step may be necessary for certain clients to get acquainted with the notion of spiritual existence. This stage was established for customers whose joys and sorrows make it difficult for them to find tranquility or feel connected to the rest of the world.

The major purpose of this stage is to assist the client in moving from a sense of incompleteness to a life filled with freedom and joy.

What makes DBT unique?

The world believes DBT can perform miracles, so why does it continue to work while other therapies, like as CBT, have failed?

DBT, like most other treatments, including CBT, fills in the gaps left by the others. CBT, for example, aims to change clients' actions and ideas to the point of horror. Most therapy for stress, anxiety, PTSD, and other issues do not encourage or assist their patients to accept where they are right now. They devalue people by claiming that their feelings are incorrect based on cognitive distortions. DBT differs in this regard.

Acceptance-based behaviors are encouraged in DBT.

Dialectical Behavior Therapy is a kind of cognitive behavioral therapy, but it is distinguished by its emphasis on dialectical thinking and mindfulness. Rather than addressing symptoms as problems to be solved, this treatment incorporates acceptance-based actions that place equal focus on acceptance of experience.

Dialectical thinking is a philosophical position in which two seemingly contradictory truths or concepts exist at the same time. A person seeking assistance, for example, must accept where he or she is currently while simultaneously having the desire to improve.

Simply said, while DBT aids in the development of acceptance, it also teaches people that they have the ability to produce more positive and perform much better. This is something that can only be accomplished via DBT.

DBT is an emotion-focused therapy.

DBT is a powerful type of treatment that entails acquiring cognitive and emotional skills and putting them into practice in your daily life. It aids in the management of uncomfortable and challenging emotions, as well as the improvement of emotional regulation. You can better regulate and express your emotions by strengthening your emotion regulation.

DBT helps people enhance their abilities by teaching them new ones.

DBT differs from other techniques in that it focuses on teaching clients specific behavioral skills in order to improve their skills. In a classroom setting, skills training is provided. A group leader is designated to each class, and his or her major responsibility is to teach various skills through classroom activities, lectures, and homework assignments.

These homework assignments assist the client in applying classroom concepts to real-life situations. Each week, groups gather for around 2.5 hours to talk about what's going on in their life. A person will require an average of 24 weeks to complete the curriculum. The curriculum can sometimes be repeated to make a one-year program.

DBT skill training is divided into four phases, each of which aids the client in achieving life stability. These modules include the following:

Mindfulness is a skill that allows you to be aware of and present in the moment.

Stress Tolerance is a talent that allows you to tolerate suffering rather than changing the circumstances in challenging conditions.

Interpersonal Effectiveness: the capacity to ask for what you need and learn to say no without jeopardizing your self-esteem or relationships.

Emotional regulation is the capacity to control the feelings that you desire to modify.

But how might people benefit from learning these skills?

To cope with a scenario or handle a challenging problem, people engage in problem behaviors. While such behaviors may give a quick fix or temporary respite, they are rarely helpful in the long run. DBT understands this and considers that patients are doing everything they can, but that they must also learn new behaviors in circumstances that are meaningful to them.

DBT aids these patients in the development of the following four behavioral skills: Emotion Regulation,

Stress Tolerance, Mindfulness, and Interpersonal Effectiveness are all aspects of emotional regulation. These abilities assist customers in identifying and overcoming obstacles in their daily lives.

Individual treatment using DBT boosts motivation.

DBT is a type of customized treatment that focuses on increasing clients' motivation and assisting them in applying the skills they acquire to deal with specific life circumstances. It's a novel strategy that allows people to accept their flaws while also motivating them to get up and do better, rather than treating them as victims who want sympathy.

DBT allows for generalization.

To assist clients in the moment of need, DBT incorporates phone coaching and other forms of coaching. The purpose is to demonstrate how to apply DBT skills to deal with challenging circumstances as they happen.

In contrast to typical therapy sessions, therapists are constantly ready to help clients through challenging situations.

Case management is how DBT structures the environment.

Case management tactics are included into DBT to assist clients in managing their own lives, including their social and physical settings. To enable the client to analyze their problems without outside assistance, therapists employ the same validation, problem-solving, and dialectical strategies. This helps him to deal with his difficulties on his own, unless it is really essential to seek the help of a therapist.

How does DBT work?

The client and therapist sit down together and establish plans to create a life worth living, which is the core purpose of DBT. Then they establish their objectives and expectations.

A typical DBT treatment plan includes five elements: a skills group, individual therapy, skills coaching, case management, and a consulting team. The standard program is described in this section.

Weekly group sessions for teaching and learning behavioral skills are done under the supervision of a therapy group facilitator and run roughly 2.5 hours. They're run like courses, with homework assigned so that patients may put their new abilities to the test.

The full curriculum takes twenty-four weeks to complete, and it may be repeated for a one-year program. A shorter section of this curriculum may be taught depending on the scenario and the patient's needs.

The DBT skill modules.

The purpose of this group skills training is to help clients better deal with the difficulties and obstacles they confront in their everyday life. These four skill modules teach them:

1. *a state of thought* (being aware of oneself and the situation we are in),

2. *ability to cope with stress* (learning how to bear our pain in difficult situations),

3. *interpersonal effectiveness* (aggressiveness and respect for others), and 4. emotional regulation (learning how to change our negative emotions).

4. *Mindfulness and distress tolerance* are part of DBT's acceptance approach, whereas interpersonal effectiveness and emotion control are part of the transformation strategy.

Individualized treatment

An individual psychotherapy session's purpose is to boost a patient's motivation. Personal issues and challenges are explored, with the therapist encouraging the patient in light of DBT's acceptance and change-oriented approach. The skills that were learnt in group sessions are reinforced. Furthermore, between the therapist and the patient, a genuine connection of mutual aid develops; the therapist becomes a true collaborator in the process, rather than merely a teacher or observer.

Individual treatment sessions operate concurrently with group training, just as they do with group training.

Coaching for Skills

When issues emerge, DBT patients can phone their therapist at any time of day for advice. Skills coaching's purpose is to teach patients how to practice and use the skills they've learnt throughout their life.

Management of Cases

It's all about assisting patients in taking control of their life. The therapist gives advice but only intervenes when it is absolutely essential.

The consulting group

Therapists are part of a consultation team that provides them with assistance for their work. They will remain motivated and competent in this manner. In stressful situations, this type of emotional support is very important.

Dialectical Behavior Therapy clients frequently have many behavioral issues that need to be addressed, not just one. The therapist must next assign a priority to the issues based on the following hierarchy: (1) a threat to one's life, (2) an impediment to therapy, (3) an impediment to one's quality of life, and (4) the need to learn new skills. Suicidal ideas, for example, are handled first, followed by alcohol misuse.

Finally, DBT contains three to four therapy periods. The patient's first out-of-control existence is represented by Stage 1. Stage 2 relates to the continuation of quiet suffering after some level of control has been attained. Setting objectives, developing self-respect, and finding happiness are all part of Stage 3's struggle. Stage 4, which is only required by a few people, corresponds to the desire for greater fulfilment and fullness via spirituality.

So, does it work?

Yes, it's a resounding yes. DBT is a research-based treatment that has been proved to be beneficial for the numerous mental diseases for which it is prescribed. It's also been proved to be successful with individuals of all ages, genders, sexual orientations, and races, and it's already being utilized in more than 25 nations.

Applications

DBT is most useful for persons who have a lot of strong emotions. They often believe their emotional responses are out of control as a result of life and relationship difficulties. As a result, people frequently act rashly in order to briefly alleviate some of their anguish. However, in the long term, their reactions tend to cause more issues.

DBT was developed to assist persons who had been diagnosed with borderline personality disorder (BPD). For these patients, this was and continues to be an extremely beneficial type of therapy. However, in recent years, DBT has been utilized extremely successfully with other people who have significant mood swings and are unable to cope with these powerful and rapid emotional urges using coping skills. Major depression, PTSD, eating disorders, severe obsessive-compulsive disorder, bipolar disorder, ADHD, anger management, and/or substance addiction affect many of these people. Many persons who utilize DBT also cope with self-injury, as this treatment has been shown to be particularly successful in addressing such emotional issues.

Let's look at the precise features that many of the people who perform well with DBT have in order to understand more about them. People that respond well to DBT have a lot of emotional sensitivity. This indicates they have a proclivity for reacting to and intensely feeling emotions. They are sometimes simply born with the ability to experience emotions more strongly than the normal individual. In reality, according to DBT theory, an emotionally susceptible person's autonomic neurological system responds to relatively modest amounts of stress. When the stressor is eliminated, their neurological system takes substantially longer to recover to normal. Furthermore, some people suffer from mood disorders such as severe depression or generalized anxiety, which are difficult to treat with medicine and have an impact on the intensity with which they perceive their emotions. As a result, emotionally susceptible persons are more likely to experience quick, strong, and difficult-to-control emotional reactions. As a result, they spend the rest of their lives on a roller coaster ride.

Clinicians have discovered, however, that the majority of emotionally susceptible persons who seek DBT treatment aren't only prone to have more strong emotions or mood disorders. They are also often exposed to depreciating situations for long periods of time. Such situations are most common in early infancy, although they can occur at any age. They didn't have the support, attention, respect, or understanding they needed to effectively process their emotions in these settings. Degrading situations can vary from serious emotional or physical abuse to parent-child relationships with improper personalities. Consider the introverted youngster who was born or adopted into a household full of extroverts and is continually mocked for it. Maybe it's the youngster with ADHD who has a rigid mother and stepfather who yells at him all the time. Both of these are instances of a negative environment. If a person who is predisposed to more strong emotions is placed in an atmosphere that does not support or recognize their feelings, they may become even more sensitive emotionally. They may subsequently become even more emotional as a result of their unintended learning that they will only be taken seriously if they display intense emotional behavior.

Borderline Personality Disorder

People with borderline personality disorder (BPD) feel emotions more strongly and for longer periods of time than the general population. Many psychiatrists describe these patients as being in a perpetual state of crisis because they have frequent and chronic outbursts. They are almost always in crisis mode since they haven't learned to adequately control their strong emotions.

People with BPD are emotionally fragile, and it takes them a long time to recover after a traumatic incident. Furthermore, therapists have observed that patients with BPD tend to adopt the same belief system as the devaluing environment to which they are exposed. This causes them to deny their own sentiments and abilities to handle issues, resulting in "self-devaluation." They also have a tendency to have high expectations of oneself and experience intense guilt and wrath when they fail to meet their objectives or face setbacks.

Another trait of persons with BPD is their proclivity for placing inflexible and unreasonable demands on themselves and others. They frequently resort to "blame" when things do not go as planned or intended. Many persons with BPD have a mental fault called blame. They blame everyone and everything for their difficulties, and they have a hard time admitting that personal behavioural adjustments are required to transform their life.

People who suffer from BPD have poor self-esteem and have trouble maintaining interpersonal connections. They like to find someone who will take care of their issues and fix them for them so that they can withdraw and not have to act on their own. They do, however, prefer to put on a competent mask so that people believe they are capable of fixing their own problems and managing their powerful emotions. They may have mastered particular aspects of their lives, but they have not been able to translate their skills to other areas.

Most persons with BDP endure considerable trauma on a regular basis as a result of the lifestyle they have established for themselves, as well as their difficulties returning to baseline following an emotional incident. They also avoid unpleasant feelings because they lack the ability to self-regulate beneficial negative emotions. As a result, individuals are unsure what to do when confronted with an emotional scenario they cannot tolerate, resulting in an intense and extended emotional state.

To deal with the extreme emotional suffering, people with borderline personality disorder may turn to cutting or other self-injurious and suicidal actions. Suicidal or habitually self-harming people are prone to emotional sensitivity. When subjected to significant trauma, such as physical or emotional abuse, the individual becomes emotionally reactive and begins to consider suicide. They eventually attempt suicide and are admitted to the hospital to rid themselves of the excruciating anguish. They are given a lot of attention here, and they feel noticed and treated seriously for the first time.

Consider a little youngster who injures himself by cutting or burning himself because it gives him brief relief. When others learn about it, they begin to take him seriously. He finally feels validated, as in the first scenario.

What do you think will happen in each of these scenarios? Both guys continue to engage in these actions over time since it is the only way they feel acknowledged and supported. It develops into a firmly entrenched coping mechanism.

Eating disorders

A medical condition in which a person's eating habits are deemed irregular is known as an eating disorder. However, an eating disorder is more than just an issue with food intake; the individual suffering from it generally has a severe problem with their body weight and/or figure. People with eating disorders may start eating much less and get preoccupied with exercise in attempt to control their looks and feel better about themselves. This mental and behavioral disease can affect both men and women and has severe consequences for the affected person's physical and emotional well-being.

Although eating disorders can strike at any age, they are most common in adolescence or early adulthood, and they frequently co-occur with other psychological and behavioral problems such drug misuse, mood disorders, and anxiety disorders. Below are the three most frequent forms of eating disorders.

Anorexia nervosa is a kind of anorexia.

Anorexia nervosa patients frequently have a great fixation with their weight. They are terrified of gaining weight and frequently refuse to maintain a healthy weight due to their bad and unrealistic body image. Many persons with this illness severely restrict their food intake to the point that they are unable to maintain their health. They continue to think of themselves as overweight even though they are physically underweight and their look causes others concern. Anorexia can result in infertility, cardiac difficulties, organ failure, brain damage, and bone loss, among other issues. People who have this condition have a high mortality rate.

Nervosa Bulimia sufferers are frequently afraid of becoming overweight and dissatisfied with their physical appearance. A cycle of binge eating is followed by overcompensation for binge eating in this condition. A person may, for example, overeat in one sitting and then resort to forced vomiting, excessive exercise, excessive laxative and diuretic usage, or any combination of these compensatory behaviors. Because sufferers are often filled with shame, remorse, and a lack of self-control, the cycle takes place in secret. Bulimia can also induce gastrointestinal issues, dehydration, and cardiac difficulties as a result of an electrolyte imbalance produced by the eating-purging cycle.

Binge Eating Disorder (BED) is a type of eating disorder in which

People who battle with binge eating frequently lose control of their food, but they do not purge like bulimia sufferers do. As a result, many people who have binge eating disorders also have obesity disorders, which can lead to health concerns including heart disease. People who deal with this illness, like those who fight with other eating disorders, frequently experience severe emotions of shame, guilt, humiliation, and a sense of losing control.

Eating disorders are theorized to originate in a variety of ways, as the disorders are often extremely complicated. Biological, psychological, and, of course, environmental elements all play a role in the development of an eating problem. These elements include:

Biological variables such as a hereditary susceptibility and abnormal hormone activities.

Deficiencies in nutrition

Psychological issues such as poor self-esteem and a negative body image

A dysfunctional family unit, for example, might be influenced by the environment.

Modeling, for example, is an occupation and a vocation that promotes extreme thinness.

Gymnastics, wrestling, long-distance running, and other sports that emphasize slenderness for performance reasons

Sexual abuse as a child

The pressure to be skinny from family, peers, and the media Transitions and life changes

Some of the signs and symptoms that may suggest an eating disorder are listed below:

Even when underweight, chronic and excessive dieting is harmful.

Obsession with calorie consumption and food fat content

Eating behaviors that are ritualistic. Eating alone, chopping up food, and concealing food for later consumption are examples of these practices.

A craving for eating. Some persons with eating problems cook delectable, sophisticated meals for others but refuse to eat them themselves.

Depression and lethargy are common symptoms of eating disorders.

Although DBT has been shown to be effective in the treatment of eating disorders, patients may require additional assistance in the early phases of treatment. This extra help might include seeing a doctor to address any health concerns and working with a dietician until their weight is stable. The dietician will often create a personalized dietary plan to assist them in regaining a healthy weight.

Bipolar disorder is a mental illness that affects people in

Because sufferers tend to alternate between manic and depressed states, this illness is commonly referred to as manic-depressive disorder. Unusual and dramatic fluctuations in activity levels, energy levels, mood, and capacity to execute ordinary tasks define this disease. Symptoms differ from regular mood swings in that they are intense and often so severe that patients might harm their relationships, imperil their work and school performance, and even consider suicide.

Bipolar disorder, like the majority of mental illnesses, has no one etiology. It's frequently a disease caused by a mix of biological and environmental causes. Many variables interact to cause the sickness or raise the likelihood of it occurring.

Bipolar disease appears to have a genetic component, since research has discovered many genes that are more likely to impact the disorder's development. Children from specific families or those who have a sibling with the condition are more likely to get the disorder themselves, according to other study.

Environmental variables, on the other hand, appear to have a significant influence in the development of the condition, according to study. In investigations of identical twins, when the siblings have the exact same genetic makeup, one twin often gets the illness while the other does not. This shows that environmental factors are at work, rather than just genetics.

People with this illness have "mood episodes," which are intense emotional states. Each episode might last anywhere from a few days to several months. Each episode depicts a significant departure from the person's usual conduct. The "manic" episode is characterized by an exceptionally happy, euphoric feeling accompanied by increased activity. The "depressive" episode is characterized by a melancholy, dysphoric, hopeless, and occasionally angry and explosive condition. When behavioral elements of both a manic and depressive episode are present at the same time, it's called a "mixed state."

Here are some signs and symptoms of bipolar disorder:

The signs of a manic episode include:

The sensation of being "high" for an extended length of time, which appears as an excessively happy mood.

Rapld speech and bouncing from one thought to the next. This is an indication that your thoughts are rushing.

The ability to be easily distracted

Excessive activity and the taking up of a large number of new initiatives.

Restlessness

Sleep deprivation

Unrealistic ideas about what you can accomplish

Impulsivity and an obsession with enjoyable and potentially dangerous actions

A depressed episode has the following characteristics:

Irritability for long periods of time

Long periods of melancholy or despair

Loss of interest in things that formerly piqued a person's attention

Fatigue and a sluggish sensation

Remembering, focusing, and making judgments are all difficult tasks.

Changes in eating, sleeping, and other behaviors are all possible.

Suicidal thoughts, gestures, and/or attempts are also possible.

Even if a person's mood fluctuations are modest, bipolar illness might develop. Some patients with bipolar illness, for example, suffer from mild hypomania. During a hypomanic episode, the person may feel wonderful and even be highly productive. Despite the fact that they are functioning normally, their friends and family detect a significant difference in their mood. The shift in mood is so striking that relatives and friends question if it's a sign of bipolar illness. If a person does not receive adequate therapy, hypomania can rapidly progress into full mania or signs of bipolar illness.

As previously stated, bipolar disorder can also manifest as a mixed state. When a person has both depression and mania at the same time, this is known as bipolar disorder. In a mixed condition, a person may get agitated, experience sleep difficulties, lose appetite, and even consider suicide. This mood may make people feel hopeless or melancholy while also making them feel incredibly energized.

Psychotic symptoms such as delusions or hallucinations can arise during a severe episode of depression or mania. Psychotic symptoms tend to reveal and amplify a person's heightened mood. If a person exhibits psychotic symptoms during a manic episode, they may imagine they are the president of a country, have vast money, or possess exceptional abilities. In a depressed episode, she may believe she is homeless, wrecked, impoverished, or a criminal on the run, among other psychotic symptoms. Because of their mood-related hallucinations, patients with this disease are frequently mistaken as having schizophrenia or another reality testing disorder.

People with bipolar illness are more likely to misuse or be dependent on various drugs at the same time. Post-traumatic stress disorder (PTSD) and phobias are both frequent anxiety illnesses. Attention-deficit/hyperactivity disorder (ADHD) and bipolar disorder are occasionally seen together (ADHD). Diabetes, headaches, thyroid disease, heart disease, migraines, and other physical problems are more common in people with bipolar disorder.

Bipolar disorder typically appears in late adolescence or early adulthood. Symptoms may first arise in childhood for some people, while others may develop symptoms later in adulthood. The sickness strikes at least half of all people before they reach the age of 25.

Bipolar disorder might worsen if it is not detected and treated. As the incidents grow more frequent, the severity increases. This delay can lead to actions that have a negative influence on relationships, personal objectives, finances, housing, employment, school, and a variety of other areas. DBT has been shown to assist persons with this condition live happier, healthier lives. DBT has helped many people minimize the severity and frequency of their episodes.

Post-traumatic stress disorder (PTSD) is a type of anxiety illness that occurs (PTSD).

People are driven to flee danger by a built-in and naturally occurring mechanism in their bodies. The fight-or-flight response is the name for this system. Your body goes into automatic reaction mode when your brain receives the warning that danger is approaching. When you're terrified, your body changes to either abandon the circumstance for safety or fight to protect your survival and self-preservation. Your dread of risky circumstances causes numerous unconscious and split-second changes in your body, preparing you to run or fight in a particular situation. This is a physiologically built-in procedure that helps people defend themselves from danger. However, repeated stress or a particularly traumatic encounter might cause this typical "fight or flight" reaction to go haywire in certain people. Post-traumatic stress disorder occurs when this process is disturbed, causing people to feel worried or afraid even when they are no longer in danger (PTSD).

PTSD frequently develops after someone has been through a traumatic and/or life-threatening event. Usually, the experience entails some form of physical suffering or danger of bodily injury. The person or a loved one may be the target of the harm or threat, or the person may have witnessed a harmful event that occurred to another person or group of people. The following are some instances of circumstances that might lead to PTSD:

War

Sexual assault or rape

Terrorism

Robbery

Train derailments

Accidents in automobiles

A plane has crashed.

Floods, earthquakes, and storms are examples of natural catastrophes.

Physical maltreatment as a child

Domestic violence is a serious problem.

Situations involving hostages

Torture

Bombings

Any other unpleasant experience

A mix of genetic and environmental variables contribute to the development of PTSD. The way a person's brain is organized to deal with fear and memories plays a big role in the development of PTSD. People with PTSD are more likely to be emotionally susceptible to anxiety as a result of their brain chemistry.

Environmental variables have a part in the development of PTSD as well. Childhood trauma, a brain injury, or a family history of mental illness can all raise the likelihood of developing the disease. Thinking mistakes, stress tolerance, pessimism, and other cognitive-related characteristics, as well as personality and cognitive traits, all enhance risk. Similarly, social variables such as the presence of a support system aid in the adaptation to trauma and may assist people avoid developing PTSD.

PTSD signs and symptoms

TSD symptoms are divided into three categories:

1. re-experiencing symptoms

Flashbacks.

The tragedy has given me nightmares.

Embarrassing ideas that invade and persist. They arise out of nowhere and are extremely tough to remove.

Re-experiencing symptoms may obviously be quite disruptive to one's everyday life. They have the potential to produce issues in a person's everyday life as well as interpersonal interactions.

2. Avoidant symptoms

When a person avoids anything that reminds them of the traumatic incident, these symptoms appear. They avoid them because being near them causes an out-of-control emotional reaction.

Emotional numbness is another avoidance characteristic. Instead of risking experiencing a strong unpleasant emotion, they experience numbness. They strive to prevent bad feelings by avoiding emotional experiences.

Another avoidance sign is experiencing severe concern, despair, or guilt without knowing why. People with PTSD may have more overall bad sentiments rather than dealing directly with their reaction to the occurrence.

Victims may lose interest in previously enjoyed activities. PTSD is characterized by the avoidance of all enjoyable activities.

It's also normal to have trouble recalling the risky occurrence. It is often simpler to simply shove the entire event into the subconscious rather than coping with what transpired. This is a case of avoidance behavior in action.

Changing routines is another method of avoidance. People with PTSD may purposefully alter their routine in order to avoid having to deal with a trigger. A person who avoids driving following a life-threatening vehicle accident is an illustration of this. This was extremely frequent following the terrorist assault on 9/11, when many passengers refused to board an aircraft.

3. Hyperarousal symptoms

People recuperating from PTSD are more likely to be startled and agitated than they were before the traumatic occurrence.

They have problems sleeping and managing their anger since their autonomic nerve system is more active. They may have frequent rage outbursts.

It's worth noting that hyperarousal symptoms are frequently persistent and occur even when there's no obvious cause. After a stressful event, it is totally typical for someone to suffer one or more of these symptoms.

Keep in mind that when a kid or teenager has PTSD, they may act in a different way. You may see the following in young children:

After they've been potty trained, they continue to pee the bed.

After they have achieved a verbal developmental stage, they do not talk.

During play, reenacting the horrific occurrence

Symptoms that are more consistent with adult symptoms may be seen in older children or teenagers. However, you may notice a rise in obnoxious and rude conduct. They may also be concerned with avenging themselves or feeling guilty for not doing more to avoid the incident or the harm that resulted from it.

PTSD may strike anybody at any age. Women are more likely to get PTSD than males, and there appears to be a significant genetic relationship. Not everyone who is exposed to a potentially dangerous incident develops the disease.

There are a number of elements that influence whether or whether a person develops PTSD. Risk factors are elements that raise the possibility of a person developing PTSD. Resilience variables are factors that reduce a person's chances of acquiring PTSD. Some of these risk and resilience variables exist before to the trauma, while others emerge during or following the trauma.

PTSD resilience characteristics include:

After a traumatic event, you should have access to an adequate support system.

A successful coping method

When issues develop, having a solid knowledge of one's own behaviors is essential.

Adjustment therapy or psychotherapy after a traumatic event

The following are some of the risk factors for PTSD:

Having a traumatic experience

Personal experience with mental illness

Injury to the body

Witnessing the deaths or injuries of others

Following an incident, there is insufficient or no social assistance.

Loss of a loved one, a house, or a job

Obsessive-compulsive disorder (OCD) is a mental illness that, if left untreated, can lead to serious consequences. It drives patients to engage in a never-ending cycle of repetitive activities and thoughts. They are swamped with uncontrollable thoughts, anxieties, and pictures. Instead, they are enamored with them at all times. Anxiety is caused by these constant and unpleasant thoughts, which makes patients feel compelled to follow specific rituals, habits, or safety-seeking behaviors. The patient seeks to remove the anxiety that comes with obsessive and repeated thoughts by engaging in these compulsive actions.

Although the ritualistic practice reduces anxiety briefly, it becomes a persistent problem when the obsessive thoughts recur and the individual must repeat the pattern. This cycle of OCD can have a negative impact on a person's relationships and possibly their health. It is not unusual for someone with OCD to devote hours of their time to ritual duties that they would not devote to other activities. People with OCD are often aware of their actions and recognize that their routines are unrealistic and unhealthy, but they are powerless to change them.

Obsessions that are common include:

Fear of being filthy

apprehension of harming others

The fear of committing a blunder

Fear of being humiliated

Fear of behaving in a way that is socially undesirable.

Fear of having bad or wicked thoughts

Excessive skepticism and a continual desire for reassurance

Among the most common compulsions are:

Reciting particular prayers, phrases, or sentences again and over

Hand washing, showering, or bathing on a regular basis

Following a set of rules when it comes to eating

Having a certain amount of errands to run

Refusing to shake hands or touch doorknobs

Hoarding

The causes of OCD are unknown, although research shows that, like most other mental and behavioral disorders, it is caused by a combination of environmental and biological variables.

Biologicals Factors

OCD is thought to be caused by difficulties in the networks connecting the regions of the brain responsible for planning and judgment with the part responsible for filtering physical actions, according to researchers. There's also evidence that OCD is handed down through the generations.

Environmental determinants

Some people's OCD is triggered by environmental stimuli. Symptoms might be aggravated by a variety of other circumstances. Some of these elements are:

Abuse

Change of address

Illness

Changes in employment

Bereavement of a loved one

Issues at school

Problems in relationships

According to a recent study, OCD affects 1 million children and adolescents in the United States, as well as 3.3 million adults. CBT and DBT are effective treatments for this disease.

Major Depression (Severe)

Almost everyone has struggled with sadness at some point in their life. Sadness is a common emotional reaction to adversity. However, if the sorrow is severe enough to impair performance and everyday activities, professional assistance may be required.

Major depression, also known as clinical depression, is characterized by a sad mood that lasts all day and is most noticeable in the morning. A lack of interest in relationships and routine chores is a sign of the condition, which occurs every day for at least two weeks.

The following are some of the most common signs and symptoms of serious depression:

Fatigue

Indecisiveness

Having a guilty conscience

Concentration has dropped.

Hypersomnia or insomnia

Sluggishness or agitation

Suicide or death thoughts on a regular basis

Gaining or losing weight

Nearly 10% of the population over the age of 18 in the United States suffers from serious depression. According to some estimates, between 20% and 25% of all individuals in the United States will suffer from serious depression at some point in their life. Older people, teenagers, and children are all affected by major depression. Unfortunately, among these populations, the illness is frequently undetected and mistreated.

Nearly twice as many women as males have been diagnosed with serious or clinical depression, indicating that more women are likely to be receiving treatment. Hormonal changes, pregnancy, miscarriage, and menopause have all been linked to an increased risk of breast cancer. Environmental stresses such as increasing stress at home or work, balancing family and career, and caring for an elderly parent are among variables that enhance the likelihood of clinical depression in women who are biologically sensitive. It's also been proven that being a single parent raises the chance of depression.

One of the reasons why women experience serious depression at a higher rate than men is because males are less inclined to disclose symptoms. Men, in particular, are notoriously under-reported when it comes to significant depression. Men with severe depression, however, are less likely to seek therapy or even communicate about their feelings.

The symptoms of depression in males differ from those in women. Here's what you may anticipate:

Anger and irritation are on the rise.

Abuse of drugs and alcohol

Violent conduct, both internally and externally (due to repressed feelings)

Unpredictable conduct

The state of one's health has deteriorated.

Suicide and murder rates are higher.

Here are a few examples of frequent triggers:

Separation, divorce, or death have all resulted in the loss of a loved one.

Moving, graduating from school, changing employment, obtaining a promotion, retiring, and raising children are all major life transitions.

Isolation from others

Relationship issues with a partner or a boss

Divorce

Emotional, sexual, or physical abuse are all forms of abuse.

People with the numerous diseases listed in this section have a difficult time controlling their emotions. Furthermore, there is frequently a social component that adds to the disorder's expression. The purpose of DBT is to help people regulate their out-of-control emotions and behaviors by including the psychosocial components of standard CBT therapy. Two DBT models emphasize acceptance and two emphasize change, as you'll learn in the next chapters, so that the sufferer feels both validated and driven to make the required behavioral adjustments.

Chapter 10
Mindfulness

Mindfulness is defined as being aware of one's surroundings and present in the current moment. There are several aspects to being aware. Observing, describing, and engaging in the present moment are all part of it. What does it mean to act in this manner? It entails not allowing your thoughts to stray. Return it to the present moment.

Even if you don't have BPD or any mental illness, mastering mindfulness and living in the now without thinking about the future or the past is a valuable skill to have.

The core psychotherapy practice of mindfulness is used to treat anxiety, anger, sadness, and other mental health issues. It has its origins in Eastern cultures' mysticism, but it has also been thoroughly researched by Western science. Mindfulness meditation is even recommended by psychotherapists for patients with specific mental health issues. Mindfulness training is an important component of CBT, DBT, and ACT (Acceptance and Commitment Therapy). It is, in fact, one of DBT's four skill modules. In a nutshell, mindfulness is a state of mind that we may obtain by focusing our attention on the present moment. This involves accepting our feelings, sensations, and ideas with peaceful acceptance.

Focusing on the present moment may appear simple to some, but it is far more difficult to do. Our minds might wander, we can lose touch with the present moment, and we can even become engrossed in obsessive thoughts about events in the past or concerns about the future. However, no matter how far our minds wander from the present, mindfulness may quickly bring us back to what we're doing or experiencing.

Even while it's natural for us to be attentive at all times, effective ACT strategies that you'll discover later may help us build mindfulness even more.

Meditation is frequently connected with mindfulness. Meditation is a powerful tool for cultivating awareness, but there's more to it than that. Mindfulness is a type of present-moment awareness that may be practiced at any time. It's a state of consciousness that you may reach by focusing on the current moment without making any judgments.

Elements

Mindfulness is made up of two key components: attention and attitude.

Attention

Many of us suffer from "monkey mind," in which our minds act like a monkey hanging from one branch to the next. Our minds go back and forth, and we typically have no clue where the concept originated from.

The monkey mind is prone to dwelling on the past and ruminating on what occurred or what might have occurred if you had done differently. It also looks into the future and speculates on what could occur. If you feed the monkey mind, it will steal you of your present-moment experience.

Remember that mindfulness entails concentrating your attention on the present moment.

Attitude

The pillars of mindfulness are non-judgment and kindness. As a result, a fully aware person understands how to accept reality rather than fighting it. This may appear straightforward, but if you begin to practice mindfulness, you'll notice how frequently we evaluate ourselves and our thoughts.

Here are some expressions we use to evaluate ourselves and others:

I'm not very good at this.

My shirt is a shambles.

My current residence does not appeal to me.

I despise my next-door neighbor.

What an irritable waitress.

Mindfulness is also the practice of controlling our inner critic. It enables us to let go of our inner expectations and accept things more fully in the present moment. But keep in mind that this does not negate the need for reforms.

Remember that you're merely deferring your judgment to give yourself more time to consider the matter and take action. The primary difference is that you may make adjustments while you are in an optimum frame of mind rather than when you are stressed or tense.

Mindfulness also encourages you to be more sympathetic with yourself, accept your experiences, and care for people around you. It also helps you to be more patient and forgiving of yourself if you make a mistake. You can remodel your brain to be nicer and more compassionate by practicing mindfulness.

How mindfulness can reshape your mind

It was once thought that the human brain could only develop up to a particular period, generally between early infancy and puberty. Various studies have demonstrated, however, that our brains can remodel themselves by establishing new neuronal connections. This is referred to as neuroplasticity, and it has essentially no boundaries.

The ancient assumption that the human brain is a static, unchanging organ has been debunked by neuroscientists. They revealed that the human brain can compensate for any damage caused by aging, sickness, or accident by reconstructing itself. Simply put, our brain has the ability to heal itself.

Mindfulness has also been shown to have a positive impact on brain growth in studies. It aids the process of neuroplasticity in particular. It's incredible to think that neuroplasticity and mindfulness can help us transform our emotions, feelings, and mental processes.

Three major studies have demonstrated how mindfulness may reorganize the human brain via neuroplasticity.

Memory, learning, and other cognitive skills can all benefit from mindfulness.

Although mindfulness meditation is linked to feelings of physical relaxation and peace, proponents suggest that it may also help with learning and memory.

Mindfulness can aid in the treatment of depression.

Mindfulness can aid with stress reduction.

the body's ability to cope with stress.

Other benefits

Aside from the advantages listed above, mindfulness meditation has other advantages for our emotional, mental, and physical well-being.

Emotional Advantages

We can be more compassionate when we practice mindfulness. Mindfulness meditation practitioners see changes in regions of the brain connected with empathy.

We become less reactive to our emotions as we practice mindfulness meditation. Mindfulness lowers the size of the amygdala, which is responsible for fear, anxiety, and aggressiveness, according to a study done at Massachusetts General Hospital.

When left to its own devices, our brain is prone to negative ideas, which mindfulness meditation may help us avoid.

Today, mindfulness is also utilized to treat anxiety and depression symptoms. Patients suffering from depressive episodes are increasingly being prescribed mindfulness meditation by several psychotherapists.

Mindfulness has been linked to increased concentration and attention span.

Mindfulness meditation also strengthens myelin, the protective tissue that surrounds neurons responsible for sending impulses in the brain, and increases neural connections in the brain.

Physical advantages

Our sympathetic nervous system, which is responsible for our fight or flight reaction, may be deactivated by deep breathing. It also stimulates the parasympathetic nerve system, which controls our sleep and digestion.

Cortisol levels in the body are reduced by mindfulness. This stress hormone raises blood pressure and elevates stress levels.

Mindfulness has been employed in weight reduction programs because it helps our thoughts to become aware of what we are consuming.

Mindfulness is also linked to an increase in telomerase, which is considered to aid in the prevention of cellular damage.

It's been proven that mindfulness meditation boosts the creation of antibodies that fight the flu virus. This demonstrates that meditation can aid in the strengthening of our immune systems.

Being mindful of what is going on in our immediate surroundings and inside ourselves at this exact moment - our thoughts, feelings, bodily sensations, and behavior - is what mindfulness is all about. The goal of mindfulness is to prevent ourselves from becoming enslaved by these occurrences. This awareness must be non-judgmental and transient, in the sense that we must concentrate just on the facts, accept them without formulating our own judgements or ideas, and then let them go.

Assume your supervisor has publicly chastised you for your job. You know you didn't deserve it, both the criticism and the manner in which it was delivered, and you get enraged.

Instead of allowing your emotions to control you, take a step back and consider the issue. "My boss is under a lot of strain right now, and he's temperamental and easily upset. His criticism of me was unjust, and I didn't deserve it, and that's why I became furious," say to yourself, and then go on.

The following example is simply one of numerous psychological abilities connected with mindfulness; those who develop these skills do activities such as meditation and mindful walking, but we can now readily comprehend and appreciate the advantages of mindfulness just from one example.

When we use our Wise Mind - the wisdom within each of us - we recognize and acknowledge our feelings, but we respond to them rationally. It is the balance between our rational mind (when we act and behave solely on the basis of facts and reason) and our emotional mind (when our thoughts and actions are governed by our feelings).

As the above example shows, mindfulness helps us master and control ourselves, especially in sudden and emotionally intense situations where we would rather react with our emotional mind. This benefit alone has many positive long-term effects - better relationships, greater self-esteem and self-respect, better responses to unexpected crises, and fewer symptoms of anxiety.

And, more significantly, being attentive allows us to enjoy life more fully.

Mindfulness activities also train our minds, so we get greater memory, stronger attention, and faster mental processing, as well as a reduction in anxiety and more control over our thoughts.

Essentials

What are the three types of mindfulness skills? Wise Mind, "What" skills, and "How" skills are the three types of mindfulness skills.

Mind that is wise

As previously stated, this is the transitional condition between our Reasonable Mind and our Emotion Mind, in which we acknowledge and act on both our reason and our emotions.

The "What" Expertise

These abilities are a response to the question, "How do you cultivate mindfulness?"

(1) observe, (2) describe, and (3) participate are the answers.

Observe

Observing means taking a step back and looking at ourselves, especially when we are too preoccupied with our problems, and experiencing and noticing our surroundings, thoughts, feelings, and sensations we perceive. It also means taking a step back and looking at ourselves, especially to reorient ourselves when we are too preoccupied with our problems.

Describe

Describing is putting our current experience into words - defining what we are feeling, thinking, or doing - using simply facts and not our personal thoughts. For example, we can tell ourselves, "My stomach feels hungry," or "Right now, I am thinking about my mother."

Participate

We forget about ourselves and behave impulsively when we participate in whatever activity we are doing (eating, conversing, or feeling fulfilled).

The "how" abilities

On the other hand, these abilities respond to the question, "How will you cultivate mindfulness?"

"Nonjudgmental, aware, and effective are the solutions.

Nonjudgmental. With a nonjudgmental attitude, we embrace each moment as it is, including our circumstances and what we perceive in ourselves: our ideas, feelings, values, and so on.

Unanimous. Mindfulness is defined as performing one activity at a time and giving it our complete attention - whether it's dancing, walking, sitting, talking, or thinking - with the goal of maintaining our focus and concentration.

Effective mindfulness practice entails having our objectives in mind and doing whatever it takes to attain them. It also means giving it our all and not allowing our emotions to get in the way.

These core mindfulness skills are at the heart of Dialectical Behavior Therapy and support all other skills; they're called "core" mindfulness skills because there are several other skills or perspectives of mindfulness that are less commonly practiced; we won't go into detail about them, but one of these other perspectives is viewed from a spiritual standpoint and is intended for those who need additional help with mindfulness in light of their s.

Now that we've learned the skills, it's time to put them to use in activities so we can observe how they work. Below is a tiny sample of the many mindfulness tasks that have already been produced for DBT.

Meditation

Meditation's purpose is to observe the current moment in a nonjudgmental manner.

Find a peaceful spot where you won't be interrupted and meditate for at least 30 minutes each day, while 10 minutes is advised for beginners.

Sit comfortably with your back straight, arms at your sides, and hands on your thighs in a chair or a cushion on the floor.

Then, with your breathing, ground yourself in the present now by paying particular attention to the inhales and exhales, as well as the noises they generate. Try to do this for the length of the exercise.

However, your mind will inevitably wander; simply take note of them without criticizing them, and then restore your focus to your breathing.

You may also have bad sensations while meditation, which is fine; simply take note of them without criticizing them and then return your focus to your breathing.

Repeat until the timer goes off, returning to your breathing anytime you get distracted.

Walking with awareness

Walking mindfully simply means paying attention to your body and environment while walking.

First, pay attention to how your body moves and feels while you walk; pay attention to the pressure on your feet and any joint discomfort, if any; and pay attention to your heartbeat's increased rhythm.

Then pay attention to what's going on around you: what do you see, hear, and smell? Do you feel the breeze or the heat of the sun on your skin?

The 5 Senses

This is about observing your surroundings with your five senses, noticing at least one item you see, feel, hear, smell, or taste.

Breathing with awareness

You may complete this mindfulness exercise while sitting or standing; if time and location allow, sit in the lotus posture; if not, don't worry; just focus on your breathing for at least 60 seconds.

Begin by slowly inhaling and exhaling, one breathing cycle lasting about six seconds.

Remember to breathe in via your nose and out through your mouth, and to let your breathing flow naturally.

Make sure you can let go of your ideas in this exercise, as well as the things you need to accomplish today or impending tasks that demand your attention. Instead, focus on your breathing and let your thoughts go their own way.

As the air enters your body and provides you life, be aware of your breathing and focus on your awareness.

Listening with Intention

This mindfulness practice improves our nonjudgmental listening skills while also training our brain to be less distracted by assumptions and previous experiences.

The majority of our feelings are impacted by our prior experiences; for example, we may despise a song because it brings up terrible recollections of a time in your life when you were in a poor mood.

You should be able to listen to neutral noises and music with a present awareness that is not obstructed by assumptions if you practice mindful listening.

Choose music or a soundtrack that you are unfamiliar with; you may have something new on your playlist, or you may put on the radio to locate music to listen to.

Put your headphones on and close your eyes.

The idea is to suspend your judgment about the music you're listening to - the genre, the artist, and the track - and to attempt to go with the flow of the song rather than anticipating the label.

Allow yourself to be immersed in the music, even if you don't like it at first; let go of your judgment and allow your consciousness to be immersed in the sound.

Navigate the sound waves by observing the vibrations of each instrument in the song and attempting to isolate and analyze each sound in your head.

Pay attention to the voices, their tone and range, and try to separate them like you did with the musical instruments if the song includes numerous voices.

The idea is to pay attention to the music and completely engage with it without evaluating it or having preconceived notions about the music, genre, or performer; this exercise demands you to listen rather than think.

Observation with Intention

This mindfulness practice is one of the most basic, but it is also one of the most effective since it helps you to appreciate the more basic components of your environment.

This practice is intended to reacquaint us with the beauty of our surroundings, which we frequently overlook as we drive to work or walk through the park.

For a few minutes, concentrate on a natural item, such as the moon, clouds, an insect, or a tree.

Relax and attempt to focus as much as your mind will allow on the subject you've been focussing on.

Allow your mind to be swallowed up by the existence of the item as you look at it and try to examine its visual features.

Allow yourself to connect with the natural environment's purpose and energy of the thing.

Conscious Awareness

Consider something you do every day that you generally take for granted, such as brushing your teeth. This mindfulness practice is meant to increase our heightened awareness and appreciation for ordinary, everyday acts as well as the consequences they bring.

Pause for a few seconds before reaching for your toothbrush and pay attention to your presence, your sensations at the time, and what that activity accomplishes for you.

Take a few seconds to remain quiet and absorb the architecture of your doorway to the rest of the world as you open the door before venturing out into the world.

These things do not have to be tangible; for example, whenever you feel sad, take a few seconds to halt, recognize the detrimental idea, understand that people are unhappy, and then move on and let go of the negative.

It may be something as simple as pausing for a moment every time you pass a flower on your way to work to appreciate how fortunate you are to witness such a beautiful joy.

Choose a touchpoint that has a significant impact on you today, and instead of going about your everyday chores like a robot, take a few seconds to step back and establish a deliberate awareness of what you are doing right now, as well as the benefits that those actions will bring to your life.

Appreciation with Intention

In this mindfulness practice, you will notice five things in your everyday life that you typically overlook, whether they be people, events, or objects; the option is completely yours. At the end of the day, make a list of the five things you observed.

The goal of this exercise is to express thanks and appreciation for the seemingly little aspects of life, such as the things that play a role in our human existence but that we frequently overlook because we are preoccupied with the "larger and more essential" aspects of life.

There are so many of these small things that we take for granted: clean water that nourishes your body, the cab driver who drives you to work, your computer that helps you to be productive, and your tongue that allows you to enjoy your wonderful meal.

But have you ever stopped to consider what you identify with these items and what function they play in your life?

Have you ever taken a step back and examined the finer points of something?

Have you ever considered how different your life would be if these items didn't exist?

Have you ever considered how these things benefit you in your life and aid the people you care about?

Do you understand how these things function or how they came to be?

After you've identified these five things, attempt to learn everything you can about their purpose and how they came to be, so you can appreciate how they help you live your life.

Immersion with awareness

Mindful immersion is a technique for cultivating satisfaction in the current moment while letting go of persistent concerns about the future.

Instead of rushing through our daily chores in order to move on to the next item on the list, we can embrace the task and fully experience it. For example, if you need to wash the dishes, focus on the specific details of that activity; rather than treating it as a mundane task, you can choose to develop an entirely new experience by paying closer attention to every aspect of your action.

Feel the rush of water as you wash the plates; is it chilly or warm? How does the rushing water feel on your hands as you scrape the grease away?

Instead of suffering through and continually worrying about completing the activity, actively observe each step and totally immerse yourself in the process, choosing to take it beyond a routine by tuning into it intellectually and physically - and even spiritually if you are a spiritual person.

You've studied what mindfulness is, its advantages, the skills it provides, and the activities you can do to improve your awareness; as you'll discover in the coming chapters, mindfulness is useful not only in CBT but also in DBT and ACT.

Increasing our ability to be aware of every moment in our lives is a useful exercise that can help us better manage the negative feelings we experience. It is not just a treatment option for those who are affected by a mental disorder. If we learn to act wisely despite our irrational feelings and become more mindful of ourselves and the things around us, we will undoubtedly be happier and more content.

You can finally develop your ability to focus on the present and face life's challenges in a confident yet calm manner by practicing mindfulness exercises on a regular basis. You will be far less likely to succumb to bad habits and let fear of the future and negative past experiences affect you if you practice mindfulness exercises on a regular basis.

You can reshape your brain to develop a fully conscious mindset free of self-limiting thought patterns, allowing you to be fully present and focused on positive emotions that increase compassion and help you finally understand yourself and those around you.

Skills

The DBT skills module on stress tolerance recognizes that certain people have a higher tendency to exhibit negative behaviors, and that these behaviors can be overwhelming for these people, so they must be addressed right away. Such people are often overwhelmed by even the smallest amount of stress, and then develop negative behaviors. To help these people, most conventional treatment approaches emphasize avoiding painful situations.

The pain tolerance module is built around the concept of radical acceptance, which entails facing the reality of a stressful situation and accepting that there is nothing you can do about it. Patients who practice radical acceptance without fighting or judging reality are less likely to develop long-lasting and intense negative feelings.

The DBT "tolerance of stress" module includes four different skills that are designed to help people cope with difficult situations and stress without exacerbating it.

Distraction

Self-soothing

Improving the situation

Considering the advantages and disadvantages

Distraction

Distraction is a technique that allows patients to shift their focus away from troubling emotions and thoughts and toward neutral or pleasant activities, such as a hobby, a short walk in the garden, helping others, or watching a movie. These activities help clients detach from a stressful situation or troubling state of mind.

To practice the art of distraction, the abbreviation "ACCEPTS" is utilized.

Positive activities might help you get over a difficult circumstance.

Contribution – Assist others in your immediate vicinity or in your community.

Comparisons - When you're feeling down, compare yourself to those who have had a more difficult life than you, or to yourself.

Emotions - Using proper activities to elicit a sensation of happiness or humor to make oneself feel different.

Displacement - You temporarily replace your uncomfortable circumstance with something less difficult. Thoughts - Try to forget about what's troubling you and shift your thoughts to something else.

Sensations - Do something severe to make yourself feel different from what you're feeling, like eat a spicy meal or take a cold bath.

Self-Calming

The Self-Calming module is about teaching you to respect and be kind to yourself, and it includes anything that uses your five senses to help you develop a positive image of yourself, such as looking out the window at a beautiful view (seeing), listening to nature sounds like birds chirping (hearing), smelling a scented candle (smelling), tasting a hearty meal (tasting), and petting an animal (petting) (touching).

Learning to self-soothe is a crucial milestone in the stress tolerance module of DBT. When you self-soothe, you treat yourself with care, love, and compassion, which will help you build resilience and recover more quickly from tough situations.

Enhance the current situation

This skill entails using positive mental forces to improve your current image in your eyes, and it can be practiced by remembering the acronym IMPROVE.

Visualize something that soothes you to melt away the unpleasant ideas using imagination.

Meaning - This entails deriving meaning or purpose from suffering or a tough scenario; in other words, finding a silver lining in all you do. This assists the client in finding something good and learning something from every event.

Prayer - This is praying to God for strength and confidence, and it has been shown to help clients calm down and strengthen their spiritual side.

Relaxation entails actions such as listening to music, sipping warm milk, or getting a massage to help the body and stiff muscles relax.

One thing at a time - This encourages people to be mindful and focus on a neutral activity that is taking place right now.

Vacation - This is urging your customers to take a mental break from a stressful situation by picturing or doing something that makes them happy, such as going on a vacation or ignoring all phone calls for a period of time.

Encouragement entails talking to oneself in a helpful and positive manner to help you get through a challenging situation.

The skill IMPROVE assists clients in enduring frustration or distress without making it worse, with the goal of improving it. It is particularly useful for people who are stuck in hopeless situations over which they have no control, as they are unable to do anything about them and thus feel hopeless, hurt, and depressed. For many people, such a situation can feel like a constant crisis. Using the skill IMPROVE helps them overcome this stumbling block.

Concentrate on the advantages and disadvantages.

The main idea here is to help them remember how avoiding confrontation in a difficult situation has negatively impacted them in the past, and to let them realize how it would feel if they could tolerate the current stress without adopting negative behaviors.

Summary

The distress tolerance module teaches clients how to really connect with others, be open to their feelings, and respond flexibly in critical situations.

Clients are able to get through any stressful moment and reduce destructive impulses and painful feelings by practicing distraction, enhancing current moments, calming their minds and bodies, and weighing the pros and cons of a given situation. It helps them take a break and return to life in a calmer, rejuvenated, and more focused state, like a full tank of gas that can now go for miles.

DBT Emotion Regulation and Interpersonal Effectiveness

Every day, we all experience millions of emotions, which affect not only our own state of mind but also our interpersonal relationships, which in turn affect our personal and social lives. Dialectical Behavior Therapy recognizes the importance of emotion regulation and interpersonal relationships, and includes two separate modules that address these issues.

Emotion regulation is an important module of Dialectical Behavior Therapy that aims to provide clients with the skills they need to manage themselves in negative situations and focus on enhancing positive experiences. Emotion regulation refers to a complex combination of ways in which a person can manage and respond to their emotional experiences. These generally include understanding and accepting emotional experiences, the ability to rely on healthy strategies to manage and respond to emotional experiences, and the ability to use healthy strategies to manage and respond to emotional experiences.

"Either you manage your emotions or you allow them to dominate you."

Clients with high emotional sensitivity frequently fall into a vicious cycle of negativity, which is often triggered by negative circumstances. These thoughts cause a person to react with negative or heightened emotions, eventually leading to difficult choices and self-destructive behaviors, which may be followed by further negative emotions such as self-loathing or shame.

During times of emotional stress, those who have a solid hold on their emotion regulation are better able to suppress desires to engage in impulsive actions such as self-harm, physical aggressiveness, or irresponsibility.

Three objectives are included in the DBT module on emotion regulation:

1. have a deeper knowledge of your emotions 2. lessen your emotional susceptibility 3. lessen your emotional pain

Negative emotions are a normal part of life and will occur no matter how hard you try to avoid them. However, there are several ways to accept and deal with them better so that you do not remain under their control.

1. Recognizing and identifying feelings

This skill teaches clients how to recognize and name emotions. They are taught to use labels like "anxious" or "frustrated" instead of general terms like "feeling bad," because vaguely defined emotions are much more difficult to manage. Another important goal of this skill is to teach the client the difference between primary and secondary emotions.

A primary emotion refers to your initial reaction to a moment or trigger in your environment. A secondary emotion, on the other hand, refers to a reaction directed at your own thoughts, such as when you are sad because you let out your anger. These emotions are usually destructive and increase the likelihood that you will develop destructive behaviors. So it is important not only to name your primary and secondary emotions, but also to accept your primary emotion without judging yourself for having to deal with it at all.

In a typical DBT skills session, group leaders discuss common misconceptions about emotions, such as the belief that there are certain "right" or "wrong" ways to feel in certain situations. Another issue is explaining the primary purpose of emotions, which is to alert you that something around you is either problematic or useful. These emotional responses are stored in your memory and help you prepare for similar situations in the future.

2. lessen emotional fragility

The acronym PLEASE MASTER is a good way to practice this skill.

E - is for eating a nutritious and balanced diet while avoiding foods high in caffeine, fat, and sugar. PL - represents for taking excellent care of your physical health and treating illness or pain.

A - stands for abstaining from drugs and alcohol, both of which exacerbate emotional instability and are harmful to one's mental health.

S - stands for having adequate sleep on a daily basis.

E - indicates exercising every day.

MASTERY - This refers to doing a task each day that will improve your competence and self-confidence.

Clients are asked to plan more experiences that make them happy and provide positivity, such as participating in a sport or hobby, having coffee with a childhood friend, reading a good book, or any other activity that gives them individual satisfaction, as this component of emotion regulation focuses on reducing emotional vulnerability by building positive experiences and balancing negative feelings.

Customers are asked to be mindful and focused on what they are doing during these activities, and if they find it difficult to do so, they can try another activity. Planning for the future and setting goals brings positive experiences for most customers, so this activity includes planning for the future, such as changing jobs or moving to a different city.

3. alleviating emotional distress

The final part of DBT emotion regulation is reducing emotional distress, which includes the following skills:

Getting Rid of Things

Taking the opposite action

Letting go entails being fully aware of your current emotional state, naming it, and allowing it to happen rather than avoiding, fighting, or obsessing over it. To do so, take a deep breath and imagine yourself moving away from the problem; compare your emotion to a wave of water that comes and goes.

If a person is sad, he or she can try to be active, stand tall, and speak confidently, as if he or she were happy. If a person is angry, he or she can adopt a gentle tone of voice or do something good for someone.

In group therapy sessions, DBT leaders try to teach clients these skills, and they may be asked to participate in role-playing to help them apply what they've learned to their daily lives. In the end, these skills help people regulate their emotions rather than being regulated by them.

Skills for interpersonal effectiveness in DBT

The capacity to engage with others is referred to as interpersonal effectiveness. It encompasses all of the abilities you employ to:

keep an eye on your connections

Maintain a healthy balance between expectations and priorities.

find a happy medium between your "wants" and "shoulds"

Develop a sense of mastery and self-respect.

Interpersonal skills are crucial.

Interpersonal skills are a crucial aspect of DBT treatment since they teach us how to communicate with others. The quality of our social lives is determined by how we communicate with others, which has a significant influence on our general well-being, self-confidence, and self-esteem. As a result, the major objective of DBT is interpersonal efficacy. It's even taught as a second module in DBT sessions, and there are a plethora of tools and materials devoted to helping clients improve their interpersonal skills.

Clients are taught strategies that enable them engage in ordinary discussions calmly and intentionally, rather than speaking impulsively due to stress or a negative feeling, in order to interact with others. While there are other skills connected to communication and relationship, DBT concentrates on two:

1. the power to request what you require or desire 2. When it's appropriate, the capacity to deny demands.

Effectiveness (objective)

Effectiveness in relationships

In terms of self-esteem, effectiveness is important.

All of the following kinds must be examined in every situation. It's also crucial to prioritize them as needed, since this will ensure that a person is satisfied with both their interactions and the outcomes.

The purpose or primary reason behind a given contact that is directly related to a concrete consequence is referred to as "objective effectiveness." A wife, for example, may like for her husband to phone her to inform her when he is working late. The final objective of a conflict-free relationship is referred to as "relationship effectiveness." In the above scenario, the wife's first and highest goal may be harmony and emotional intimacy. In this woman's case,'self-esteem effectiveness' may also be a priority if she believes her spouse is being disrespectful by not phoning her according to her desires.

Various acronyms are used in Dialectical Behavior Therapy to assist clients master the skills associated with each type of effectiveness. DEAR MAN is the acronym of choice when it comes to objective effectiveness.

Describe the situation in precise words without making any judgments.

Express: Let the other person know how you feel about the issue by expressing your feelings and communicating them to them.

Assert: Make a strong case for what you want and what you don't want.

Reinforce: Reiterate why you desire a specific result and reward those who comply with your request.

Attentive: Concentrate on the work at hand to be mindful and focus your attention on the current moment.

Make eye contact throughout talks and be confident in your look, tone of voice, and posture.

Negotiating: Be willing to negotiate, believe in "give and take," and acknowledge that everyone participating in a negotiation has legitimate feelings and needs.

In DBT, the acronym for relational effectiveness is GIVE:

Kind: avoiding judgemental comments and assaults by approaching the other person in a non-threatening and gentle manner.

Show interest by allowing people to speak and truly listening to what they have to say. Interrupting someone only to express your own view or judgment is not a good idea.

Validate and acknowledge the wishes, ideas, and feelings of others.

Loose: Maintain a relaxed demeanor by speaking in a lighthearted tone and always smiling.

In the DBT Interpersonal Effectiveness Module, the abbreviation for self-esteem effectiveness is FAST:

To prevent generating resentful sentiments on any side, be fair to yourself and others.

Apologize less and take responsibility only when it's necessary.

Sticking to: Do not compromise your essential principles in order to get a certain result.

Honesty: Tell the truth without exaggerating or feigning powerlessness in order to influence people.

Stress Management

DBT's Distress Tolerance Skills can help you get through difficult situations without hurting yourself. They may not provide you with long-term methods, but they can assist you in learning skills that will enable you to successfully self-manage through challenging situations. You can use the following strategies to cope with high levels of stress:

Distraction

You may become engrossed in meditations and anxieties as a result of stress. Keep your mind and body engaged with an activity that diverts your attention and stops you from thinking about what's bothering you—at least for a while—and you'll have enough time to consider the stressor and how to deal with it. To take your mind off the tension, call a buddy, exercise, read your favorite book, or watch a hilarious movie.

Self-soothing

Remember to treat yourself with kindness and gentleness. It's natural to be harsh on oneself, especially when you're under pressure. You doubt your own talents and believe you are incapable of dealing with your challenges. Stress and anxiety can be relieved by including relaxing activities into your everyday routine. To relax your body, listen to peaceful music, bake cookies, enjoy a gorgeous sunset, or eat your favorite dish.

Relax as much as possible.

You must practice relaxation for both the mind and the body if you follow the stress tolerance module. Any activities that may help you relax should be tried. Take a hot shower or do some relaxation exercises. Avoid multitasking and try to concentrate solely on the current work. In your thoughts, create a relaxing vision.

Consider the advantages and disadvantages.

Make two lists of the advantages and disadvantages of a stressful scenario with a piece of paper and a pencil. Make a list of ways stress might hurt you if you don't manage it. Consider how stress might assist you in developing and growing as a person. When you're finished, look through the lists again to keep yourself motivated.

Breathe

Pay closer attention to your breathing rhythm. To concentrate your attention, try taking deep breaths or counting your breaths. This might help you relax and become more aware of your surroundings.

Summary

Because of continual stress, it's quite simple to go down a rabbit hole and lose sight of the most essential things in your life these days. Remember that you are in charge at all times, even if it means letting go of things over which you have no control. While you may not be able to address every difficulty in your life, you can certainly handle your frustrations more confidently using DBT stress tolerance abilities. Don't let stress get the best of you!

Worry Management

There is no quick fix for controlling anxiety, but there is one that does work: DBT. Worrying ideas might linger for a long time, but you can cultivate a Teflon mind with ease. It only takes a little time and effort.

Look for the canaries in the coal mine. Recognize that the worries you have are just that: worries. Although it may take some time to master this talent, it may be learned very fast. Negative emotions are the most hardest to deal with. Negative ideas lead to negative feelings, and negative emotions lead to negative thoughts, trapping you in a vicious cycle.

You tend to forget about your body while you're engrossed in disturbing thoughts. Recognize bodily symptoms such as sweating, shallow breathing, and muscular tightness that accompany your emotions.

Make a list using a piece of paper and a pen. When you're nervous, remind yourself of every tiny thing that comes to mind. Make a list of any bodily manifestations that arise during a stressful situation. This is how the canaries in the coal mine are discovered. Keep track of the acts you take when you're anxious (e.g., procrastination, drinking alcohol, etc.). Familiarize yourself with these steps so that you know what to do the next time concern comes.

Avoid avoidance at all costs.

Why should you stay away from avoidance behaviors? Because you should disprove your fears. If you continue to avoid triggers, you will just be prolonging your anxiety. When you worry and then understand that you were worried for no reason, a phenomena known as "extinction" happens, and the worrying disappears.

On the other hand, suppressing your sensations for a long time makes you believe that they are genuine and that it is reasonable to be afraid of them. This is referred to as "reinforcement," and it just adds to the anxiety.

Remind yourself that avoiding a situation is incorrect whenever your mind tells you to do so. Allow yourself to enjoy the moment, seeing it as a chance to overcome your fear and forget about your worries. Shift your focus away from your worrisome thoughts and into the actual world.

Let's move on to what you should do now that you know what to avoid.

Identify

Do you ever reflect on a worrying experience and say to yourself, "Wow, that truly worried me"? That's because you didn't see it happening at the time. Worry has a way of sneaking up on you, and when you have a cognitive fusion, worry takes control. This causes you to make poor choices. The easiest method to avoid this problem and the resulting chaos is to notice the rising anxiousness before it's too late. I'm sure you've compiled your own list of canaries by now. Great. You should now be able to spot these things when they occur. The sooner you notice these ideas, urges to act, and bodily manifestations that go along with them, the easier it will be to resist them. Once you know what you're searching for, identifying your problem is simple. You'll be able to control it, or at least get a grasp on it, this way.

Engage

Have you ever been plagued by disturbing thoughts about a specific issue, only to be confronted with a larger issue? This freshly emerged difficulty pushes you to forget about your previous tensions and focus all of your remaining energy on it. Consider how you can change your focus. However, doing it on purpose is the difficult part.

This skill's objective is to assist you in developing a connection to your feelings and experiences. Instead of spending your energy on anxious thoughts, you learn to stay in the present moment and better connect to your life this way. So, if you're in a stressful or troubling circumstance, remember to concentrate solely on the subject at hand and ignore any distracting ideas.

Concentrate all of your focus on the present moment. If anxiety distracts you, recall that point and focus solely on the situation at hand, attempting to fix it.

Look after your feelings.

You must first learn to detect anxiety before you can take care of your emotions. When you recognize you're in a bad situation, pay special attention to your body. Look for symptoms that your emotions are out of control. Your stomach may constrict, your heart may pound, and your muscles may stiffen. Pay close attention to everything you're feeling.

It's conceivable that your mind has shifted its focus to something else. You can also feel as if you're drowning in a sea of worry, diverting your focus away from the true issue. Pull yourself together if you find yourself in this circumstance. Return your whole attention to your body and concentrate on the genuine issue. Do not become engrossed in troubling ideas. Simply be aware of them and return your attention to your body. Fear, anxiety, annoyance, sadness, or humiliation are all emotions that may be named. Remind yourself that feeling the way you do is natural and that your emotions will not kill you.

Examine, acknowledge, and mark, in a nutshell. The uncomfortable sensations will fade away in time. It's an art form that takes time to master. It does, however, work. This will be your worry-fighting superpower if you grow proficient at it.

Use the inverse action.

Take it slowly because this may appear to be advanced kung fu. Finally, it is this skill that will help you go from being a chronic worrier to a person who seldom worries. It's a gentler kind of "exposure therapy" that focuses on "confronting your anxieties."

Opposing acts assist your brain in determining which persons and situations are not harmful and hence do not require avoidance. Your anxieties begin to disappear once your brain is able to form this link. You have the freedom to do and go as you wish in life when you stop avoiding people or things.

Please take a few moments to respond to the following questions:

Do you have concerns about things that aren't genuine or imminent dangers?

Do you worry so much that it's tough to relax and enjoy yourself?

Is it more probable that you will be sad than happy?

Are you afraid of taking fair risks?

Is worrying interfering with your regular routine?

If you answered no to the following questions, you are most likely in good health. So keep doing what you're doing because only actual dangers are a threat to you. To live a happy life, you will take every feasible action.

If you answered no to the majority of the above questions, you are suffering from anxiety. To remove the unwanted load from your shoulders and live, you must perform the measures outlined above.

Regrettably, there is no magic drug that can make you or your troubles disappear overnight. However, following the steps outlined above to implement DBT can make a huge impact in your life and make it simpler.

Post-Traumatic Stress Symptoms

DBT is a strong mind control strategy that teaches you how to manage with unpleasant thoughts and events that cause you to suffer. People with PTSD can learn how to survive by using acceptance and transformation strategies:

Recognize the triggers that drive you to respond negatively.

To relax their body and mind, they should engage in self-soothing activities.

Learning to deal with unpleasant sensations, events, and ideas by developing intolerance abilities

DBT (Distress Tolerance ACCEPTS) is an acronym that can help you manage with PTSD.

Activities, Contributing, Comparisons, Emotions, Push away, Thoughts, and Sensations are all part of this talent. These approaches were created to assist you in managing your emotions and moving on from your past.

Activities

Participate in an activity. Any activity would suffice as long as it is wholesome. Read a book, take a stroll, make jam, or clean your house. Anything that keeps you occupied and diverts your attention away from the bad feelings of the past will be beneficial. Take up a new hobby once you've finished. This way, you can have a productive day without having to deal with the recollections of the past.

Contribute

Make a good gesture for someone else. In many ways, offering to assist may reduce your emotional tension. A form of action that distracts you and takes your attention off your difficulty is an act of service. Furthermore, giving back might make you feel good about yourself. It is not always necessary to take on a large project. Offer to assist someone in the kitchen, bake cookies for a relative, or trim your neighbor's lawn. Any of these things will distract you from your sorrow.

Compare

It's time to take stock of your life. Have you ever experienced more challenging issues than the ones you're dealing with now? Perhaps not. This might be the most intense circumstance and emotion you've ever encountered. In that situation, make a comparison to someone else. Did that individual go through greater pain than you? Are you relaxing in your house after a nice supper, while someone in another part of the globe is hunting for leftover food in the garbage and a place to sleep following a natural disaster? The goal of this exercise is not to exacerbate your existing anguish or emotional suffering. Instead, utilize it to offer a fresh perspective to what you're going through.

Emotions

You have the ability to elicit the emotion that is the polar opposite of what you are now experiencing. A 15-minute meditation session might also help you relax. Watch an amusing movie if a former trauma is depressing you. A small amount of the opposing feeling can assist to lessen the severity of PTSD.

It should be pushed aside.

It's fine to shove your history aside if you don't feel ready to deal with it yet. For a brief while, put the subject out of your thoughts. How is this feasible, though? By diverting your attention to other things such as ideas, activities, or awareness. You can schedule a return visit to address your issues. Reassure yourself that you'll handle it, and keep your cool in the meantime.

Thoughts

Replacing worried, negative thoughts with tasks that occupy the majority of your attention, such as repeating the alphabet backwards or doing a Sudoku problem, will help you relax. These diversions will keep you from engaging in self-destructive activities or revisiting painful situations until you have reached emotional equilibrium.

Sensations

When you're stressed, employ your five senses to help you relax. Taking a warm bath with calming music and a lavender bath bomb, eating your favorite meal, or watching a nice program on TV are all examples of self-soothing activities. For the time being, anything that engages your senses might help you manage with PTSD.

These Dialectical Behavior Therapy strategies will help you cope with PTSD until you can find a permanent solution. They can help you manage your PTSD symptoms and allow you to focus more on the present without being distracted by memories from your terrible past. While ACCEPTS skills will help you focus on the present moment, DBT modules like group therapy and interpersonal effectiveness will encourage you to appreciate life on a fundamental level.

Chapter 11
Controlling Emotions

Mastery in action

You can gain Wise Mind by using the mastery talents in this area. It will be simpler for you to recall these abilities in times of turbulence if you exercise Wise Mind while the waters of life are calm.

You lessen stress and increase self-confidence by doing something each day that helps you feel a bit better. In difficult situations and in everyday life, self-confidence helps to minimize stress.

Taking care of yourself keeps you grounded so that you can retain your cool and maintain a consistent emotional level when troubles emerge, which they will.

Create happy memories.

We need a reservoir of happy experiences to draw on when we are stuck, thus building pleasant experiences is essential for mood regulation. Many events are fantastic at the time, but we may not be friends with the individuals with whom we shared them later. Allowing that to cloud your memory is not a good idea. Remember who they were at the time you shared the encounter. The short-term and long-term are two essential areas in which you might generate pleasant experiences.

Short-term

Talking with a good friend, going for a walk, seeing a beautiful neighborhood, going to the dog park, reading a good book, watching a favorite show or movie, eating at a restaurant, going on a picnic, or laughing with a coworker on a break are all examples of short-term memories. Without even realizing it, most of us already do something every day to have great short-term experiences.

This practice encourages you to purposefully generate more short-term happy experiences. Make a call to an old acquaintance. After work, stay away from social media for a few days. Make a point of telling your kids absurd, foolish stories. Send presents from the sale rack to your nieces and nephews. Make a conscious effort to accomplish something that will bring you joy.

You will begin to create and notice more positive experiences in your daily life if you consciously practice creating and noticing them. You will feel better emotionally and physically if you incorporate positivity into your daily routine.

Every day for a week, do at least one of these activities, or anything else that makes you happy. Make a week's effort to do it. After that, attempt to find a way in on your own. Make an attempt at something you've never done before. There's a good chance you've never considered the following:

a nice book to read

In the middle of the week, go out for a drink

Seeing a movie and eating a delicious meal

visit a karaoke joint

learn how to make sushi

jogging

swimming

take a whiff of the flowers

with pals, play board games

go to the movies

purchase new clothing,

receive a massage

Sightseeing

writing in a journal

spending some time alone, away from the television,

visit the sauna

Long-term

Positive experiences that last a long time are more goal-oriented and result in a life worth living. What are the objectives you'd like to achieve? Make a list of a few particular objectives. Subdivide them into subcategories.

Money

Many people have financial objectives. Make a list of how much you want to save or pay off each month. You are less likely to spend money if you put it in a location where you will forget about it, such as an IRA (Individual Retirement Account) that you cannot touch.

Learn how to create a budget. Maintain a record of how much you spend and how much you earn. Keep a record of all your outgoings. Look for places where you may save money. Slowly itemize your expenses, saving them on your phone until you can transfer them to a spreadsheet. You'll already know how much you spent on medical supplies or work-related costs when tax time arrives. Instead of using your credit card, use your debit card. Then you only spend what you have, and even if you don't retain your receipts, everything will show up on your bill.

Attempt to save as much as possible. Instead of dining out, save money by bringing your own lunch. Fill a jar with it. When your youngster requires shoelaces or similar items, use the pennies. It's fine if you forget you ever had dignity after a period of paying with change.

Relationships

1. Mend a broken relationship.

If you have a relationship that you believe has to be healed in order for you to go on with your life, you may need to take action. It's possible that you'll have to take the initiative and make the initial apology. Not a phony "I'm sorry you're upset," but a genuine "I'm sorry I treated you that way" apology. Not even a half-hearted apology - "I'm sorry I treated you that way, but you deserved it, and here's why..." If he accepts your apology, you may start a conversation.

2. Break up with someone.

Not every relationship can be saved, and not every relationship should be. It may be time to leave the relationship and move on if you have apologized sinceramente and been rejected. It may be upsetting for both of you, but some relationships become poisonous for one or both of you over time. If this is the case, you can give it one final go before calling it quits. If he returns, you may assess how you feel at the moment and if you want to continue your relationship. Some relationships might be better off if they died. The actual zombie apocalypse is resurrecting them.

3. Make new acquaintances.

It becomes more difficult to form new relationships as we grow older. To meet new individuals, we must truly leave our comfort zones. Speak with the other members of your bowling league. Starting a bowling league is a good idea. Meet new individuals at events you go to on a regular basis, such as church, kayaking, or suing people. Or even at family get-togethers.

4. Make an effort to improve your present relationships.

Work on strengthening the bonds you already have. Deepen your relationships with others. Do you have a true understanding of their aspirations, concerns, desires, and dreams?

Make an attempt to maintain contact. The majority of friendships are formed when it is convenient for both or all parties to converse or meet. Texting is an excellent method to let your pals know you're thinking about them, and they will react as soon as they are able. It's also a terrific method to communicate incorrectly, but that can happen with any media.

Mindfulness in a positive light

1. Keep pleasant events in mind.

You may cherish the present by practicing mindfulness while doing something you like. Concentrate on the good aspects of your experience and change your mind as needed. This is how you develop a mindfulness practice and learn to focus on the good parts of the day or moment. The more we concentrate on something, the more we become aware of it. That's just how our minds function. That doesn't imply it's more prevalent in reality, but it is in our heads, because we have to live somewhere, so we may as well learn to appreciate the company.

2. Do not be concerned about being concerned.

Distract yourself from thoughts like "I don't deserve this happiness," "I don't know when the good times will finish," and "I don't know what duties need to be done elsewhere." Distract yourself from worrying about what awaits you at the conclusion of the great experience or how much money you'll spend on it. When you're at the circus, for example, don't think to yourself, "I don't deserve to enjoy this," but instead concentrate on your surroundings.

3. practice.

This part is extensive, and no one expects you to master it in a single sitting. You shouldn't either. This, like any other habit, must be practiced before it becomes ingrained. Then there's the matter of practice.

Be aware of happy feelings.

Make it a practice to pay attention to your feelings, whether they're happy or negative. If they're negative, make it a point not to focus on them. Make it a practice to pay attention to the genuine feeling if they are favorable. "I am joyful right now. It feels warm. It feels serene." Instead of focusing on why you are happy, peaceful, or whatever, describe how you are experiencing.

Use the action that is the polar opposite of feeling.

When you're experiencing a bad emotion, what activities do you take? These are most likely the activities that your mind has pre-programmed for you. It takes time, but by performing the polar opposite of what you habitually do, you can reprogram your mentality. When you're terrified, your brain goes into one of three modes: fight, flight, or freeze. This is still a necessary response mechanism for our own safety in some cases. In other cases, the reaction mode was passed down from our hunter-gatherer forefathers and currently serves no purpose. Take, for example, test anxiety. It's true.

An exam does not necessitate a fight-flight-freeze response in the same way that a looming death, beating, rape, car accident, or full-grown saber-toothed tiger would. The reaction, however, remains the same, and we have little control over our subconscious reactions. However, we have the ability to select our conscious behaviors. For example, if you're worried about taking a test, try taking a lot of practice tests.

Perhaps your anxiety is like a roller coaster. To desensitize yourself, ride more often with someone you trust. Attempt to become desensitized to fear. If clowns give you anxiety, go to McDonald's more often. There are no actual clowns to deal with. These maniacs will devour you alive while you sleep.

Remove yourself from the scenario that makes you furious and conduct breathing exercises if your reaction to rage is to shout and hurl objects. Unless you're a driver, of course. Then all you have to do is practice breathing exercises.

If a certain person or politician gets you upset, try to discover a nugget of truth in what they've said to earn pity, empathy, or at the very least, avoid hatred. That's not true. Turn the television off. Work on it with a genuine person, not a politician, in your life. If self-isolation is your primary reaction to melancholy, try the opposite. Volunteering in the community is a great way to give back to the community. Spend time with your buddies. Just to get out of the home, go to an ice cream parlor by yourself. Also, enjoy some ice cream.

If you're embarrassed, the first thing you should do is ask yourself, "Why do I feel this way?" Was it because you did something you're embarrassed about? Acknowledge it to yourself and your adversaries, then move on. The longer you reject it, the longer it will remain, reinforcing other unpleasant feelings such as rage. Welcome to patriarchy if you have done nothing wrong but are dragged through the dirt for pointing out something that someone else has done. It may oppress men as well. Just keep your head up and go about your business. People will soon recognize you for who you truly are. Those who don't notice it are frequently filtered out. Allow them to do so.

Guilt, like shame, functions in a variety of ways. If you need to apologize sinceramente, do so. It makes no difference whether you refuse to do so, whether it is accepted, whether the person has offered an apology, or whether they deserved the action for which you must apologize. If you resist, you will simply widen the chasm. When the feeling is inappropriate for the situation, the opposite reaction works best. Even if you're furious about something, it's still a good idea to take a deep breath and assess the issue calmly. The other person, on the other hand, may be aware that you are upset. All the better if your rage inspires you to make a constructive change.

Chapter 12
Interpersonal Relationships

Objectivity is combined with efficiency.

D - Explain

Only use facts to describe the occurrence. Use logic instead of emotion. This is critical so that the other side knows the issue completely before you ask, request, or make a choice.

E stands for express.

Use "I feel" or other "I" expressions to express yourself. These comments allow the speaker to take responsibility while also preventing the listener from slipping into defensive mode. This is necessary so that the other person knows what you're saying when you describe your feelings about the scenario.

A - Make a claim

Assert your point of view by either asking directly for what you require or plainly explaining your viewpoint.

R stands for Reinforcement.

Ascertain that the other party understands why they should comply with your request or accept your conditions without retaliation. Relationships are built on reciprocity, thus this is crucial. It's not a huge problem if one side feels disgruntled now and again. If one party feels aggrieved more frequently, the relationship will most likely end.

M stands for mindful (stay).

Keep your attention on the discourse.

A - Exude self-assurance

Maintain a confident demeanor, regardless of how you are feeling.

N is for Negotiate.

Negotiate.

Exercises for interpersonal effectiveness

Step 1: Pick an area of your life where you'd like to improve.

Community, love, education, career, personal growth, environment, family, parenting, health, money, and other factors may be considered.

Step 2: Make SMART (Specific, Measurable, Adaptable, Realistic, and Time-Bound) goals.

Try to be as detailed as possible when describing what you intend to achieve. Make sure you understand the procedures necessary to complete the task. A precise aim is more manageable than a broad goal. If you only establish a goal to spend more time with your child, for example, you have no way of knowing if you've actually accomplished it. A more precise objective may be to spend at least one hour each day playing. You'll be able to tell if you've met your goal and track your progress if you set a specific goal.

Meaningful - Consider whether your goal is truly based on your values rather than a strict rule or a sense of obligation. If you don't believe your goals have a deeper meaning, consider whether they are truly influenced by the values that matter to you. Remember that your primary values should be founded on things that give your life significance.

Adaptable - Make sure your goal will help you move in the direction you believe will improve your life the most. Examine whether your goal is bringing you closer to or further away from your life's true purpose.

Realistic - If you set goals that are not truly attainable, you are likely to experience disappointment, frustration, and failure. Attempt to strike a balance between goals that are relatively simple to attain and those that are nearly hard to achieve. Be realistic and practical in order to make a genuine attempt to attain your objectives.

Time commitment - You may make your goals even more specific by specifying a time and date by which you wish to attain them. If this isn't possible or reasonable, attempt to establish a time limit for yourself and do everything you can to stick to it.

Step 3: Determine the importance of your objectives.

The third stage is to choose how quickly you want to attain your objective. Your objectives might be as follows:

Long-term - Make a plan with the steps you'll need to take to get closer to your objectives in the next six months to a year.

Medium-term - Think about the steps you'll need to take in the next two to three months to get closer to your goals.

Short-term - Make a list of the tasks you'll need to complete in the next month to achieve your objectives.

Immediately - What are the objectives you need to meet in the next week or perhaps the next day?

It will drive your committed activities if you begin to live in harmony with your unique fundamental ideals.

The best strategy and principles are meaningless unless they are backed up by action. Knowing what basic principles you truly wish to pursue will help you live a life of significance.

Worksheet on Personal Values

A values clarification exercise can assist you or your client in exploring and clarifying the things that are significant and essential to you. Where we put our attention and time is influenced by our ideals.

Using 10 distinct categories, this self-reflection activity will help you explore different elements of your life. Write down what is most essential to you in each department over the long run. Consider why they are significant to you and which ones you believe are the most significant.

There are ten categories in this worksheet:

What type of companion would you like in a romantic relationship? What would you say your ideal relationship is like? What qualities do you seek in a partner?

What types of things do you like to undertake for enjoyment and relaxation? What do you want to do with your spare time? What excites you the most? Relaxing?

Job/career - What are the most significant career goals for you? What kind of job are you looking for? Do you aim to be a specific type of employee? What type of professional connections do you hope to establish?

Friends - What kinds of social interactions do you think are vital to cultivate? What do you consider to be the most significant aspects of having a social life? What do you want your friends to think of you as a person?

Parenting - How do you want to be a mother or father? Are there any characteristics you'd wish to instill in your children? What would you say is the ideal relationship between you and your children?

Fitness objectives and ambitions, as well as the relevance of personal health, physical well-being, and personal cleanliness, are all addressed in these questions.

Social Engagement/Environmental Responsibility - This area include community involvement, environmental endeavors, and volunteerism.

Family Relationships - These values apply to relatives such as siblings, extended family, and so on, just as they do to parenting.

Spirituality - Religion, personal belief in anything that matters on a deeper or larger level are all relevant issues here.

Personal development and growth - Think about your own talents, competences, skills, knowledge, and growth in this category.

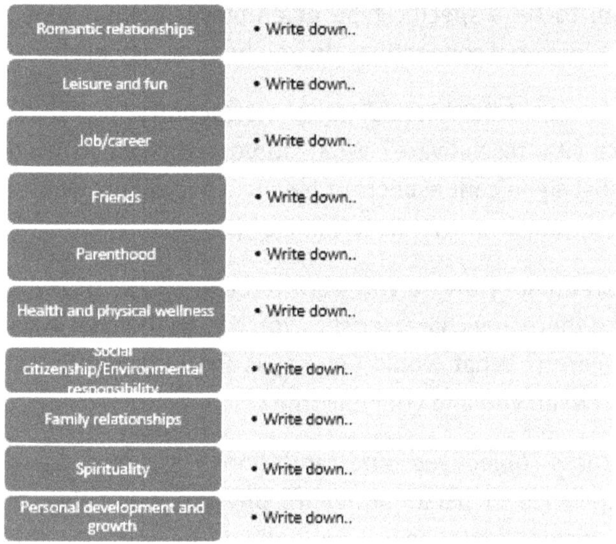

Suggestions for a better life

When trying to boost your self-esteem, stay away from putting others down. When you don't believe you're all that terrific, you have to fight the impulse to criticize others. Avoiding comparisons with others is an excellent method to master this. If you're feeling depressed, you could try to bring others down in order to feel better. If you are not competing with others, on the other hand, you are less likely to feel inferior to them. When you tear others down, the good feelings fade quickly, and you don't get a nice response from others; in fact, it frequently makes matters worse. Concentrate on your own individuality rather than comparing yourself to others.

Consider yourself superior to others. You are not superior to others, and no one else is superior to you. This is a universal fact that should be accepted by everyone. When you persuade yourself that you are better than other people, you are attempting to replace your emotions of unworthiness with the unhelpful conviction that others are not as good as you. Your relationships will suffer as a result of this inclination. Instead of attempting to persuade yourself that you are superior to others, concentrate on your own value and distinctiveness. People who are truly masterful are so confident in their own self-worth that they wish to inspire others to do the same.

People-pleasing. Chronic philanthropists frequently suffer from a deep and abiding loathing of themselves, to the point that they feel compelled to seek others' admiration. You may not be aware of your hate because it is often unconscious. You do not, however, need to wish frantically that people would like and approve of you. Whether or whether they do so has no bearing on your own worth and value.

Constructive criticism should be avoided. Everyone, without exception, has certain areas in which they might improve. This is one of the characteristics that distinguishes you as a human being. The continual growth of a person is an element of their ultimate destiny. Because self-actualization is a process, no one ever entirely achieves it. If you reject constructive criticism, you are implying that you feel you are insufficient. Change your mindset and accept the more beneficial alternative notion that good constructive criticism is necessary for everyone to break the stalemate and grow as a person. Don't be ashamed of your flaws, and don't attempt to compensate for them with perfectionism. Rather, attempt to spot them, take constructive criticism, and learn from it.

Avoid failure and rejection at all costs. If you are continuously conducting your life in a way that you believe will help you avoid failure or rejection, it is probable that you will benefit from evaluating your beliefs and implementing some healthier alternatives. Temporary failure is unavoidable at times, and rejection may surface from time to time. You must, however, learn to persevere in the face of adversity and go on, or you will become paralyzed by fear of failure and rejection.

Trying to keep emotions at bay. In the long term, attempting to conceal emotions is neither healthy nor sustainable. Being human means having a wide range of emotions, and being strong does not imply ignoring them. Allow yourself to fully feel negative emotions before employing techniques to alter the circumstance or your perception of it.

Attempt to exert influence over others. This isn't your responsibility. You don't have to establish your worth by attempting to persuade others to follow your views. Instead, concentrate on your own personal development.

You're very self-conscious about your self-esteem. No one is saying you should be a doormat for people to tread on, but if you always feel the need to defend yourself, it's a sign you're having self-confidence issues. You will not feel the need to continuously defend yourself if you are satisfied with your own self-worth. Allow yourself to not become enraged every time someone says anything negative about you or holds a different viewpoint than you. Instead, accept that you will disagree, suffer bad feelings, modify your perspective about your own self-worth, and keep working toward your objectives. It's important to remember that you can respect yourself even if other people don't.

Make excuses for your difficulties by blaming others. Of course, you've had your fair share of setbacks. In fact, more than half of the American population has been through a traumatic event, so you're not alone. Attitudes and behaviors distinguish persons who achieve their goals from those who do not. Don't blame your troubles on nature or other people. Don't put your problems down to your history, your genes, your hormones, or anything else. Concentrate on attaining your objectives rather than being side-tracked by blame.

Take yourself and your life less seriously.

Recognize that you will make errors. Because you are human, you will undoubtedly make mistakes at some time in your life. At some points in your life, you will make more mistakes than at others. The most essential thing is that you repair your errors by altering your thought and behavior habits. Expect to make errors from time to time, and recognize that they are significant because the lessons you acquire from them are crucial to your personal growth. Experiment with fresh ideas. Don't be scared to branch out and try something new. You'll gain confidence as well once you realize that attempting new things might lead to excellent outcomes. Even if you "fail," you will have gained valuable experience. When you practice self-acceptance while doing these dumb activities, you will discover that you are less likely to feel embarrassed. Make a fool of yourself. That's all there is to it. Start laughing at yourself when you have the tendency to be too critical or when you feel ashamed. Stop being so serious about yourself. Things take place. Instead of obsessing over it, learn to joke about it.

Chapter 13
Managing Stress

Everyone experiences stress at some point in their lives. However, other people claim to be extremely stressed the majority of the time. In fact, 21% of Canadians aged 12 and up consider their lives to be somewhat or severely stressful. While stress isn't always bad and may even be beneficial, too much of it can be harmful to your health.

What causes you to be stressed?

When you believe the demands of a situation or event are too much for you to handle, you are stressed. It may happen in ordinary circumstances like:

- Dealing with work or school commitments.

- Managing relationships

- Dealing with money problems

- Handling unjust treatment

- Managing long-term health issues

Stress can also be triggered by a specific incident or circumstance. Both pleasant and bad life events can be stressful, especially when they require significant adjustments in your daily routine. Some instances are as follows:

- Relationship transitions

- Modifications to your living circumstances

- The death of a close relative or acquaintance

- Job or other sources of income changes

Because stress is determined by how you perceive and respond to a circumstance or event, the events or situations that generate stress are unique to each individual.

The way you feel when difficulties emerge might have an impact on how you handle stress. A issue may not appear as worrisome if you are feeling well and confident in your ability to conquer obstacles. However, if you are already anxious or overwhelmed, the same situation might exacerbate your stress and make you feel even more overwhelmed.

Are you showing indications of being stressed?

Your body, your habits, your feelings, and your thoughts may all be affected by stress. Here are some common stress indicators:

Your body's changes

- Muscle tension

- Rapid heart rate and breathing

- Migraines

- Inability to get a good night's sleep

- exhaustion

- Modifications in sex drive

- Immune system that is weakened

Behavioral changes

- Isolation from others

- Fidgeting and restlessness

- Excessive smoking, drinking, or drug usage

- Staying away from unpleasant circumstances

Emotional alterations

- You are worried or perplexed

- You are enraged or irritated

- You feel powerless or overwhelmed

- You believe you are unable to deal

Changes in your perspective

- Inability to concentrate, recall, or make judgments

- Your self-esteem plummets

- You have a pessimistic view of yourself and your life.

Why do I feel so bad when I'm stressed?

Emotional anguish is a sort of mental tension. Your body is programmed to respond to stress in a way that protects you against predators. Although life-threatening predators are less prevalent nowadays, you still have numerous obligations to meet on a daily basis, such as paying bills, working, and caring for your family.

The fight-flight-freeze reaction is triggered in your body when these requests are seen as threats. Stress can sometimes have a detrimental impact on mental health's fundamental characteristics (your thoughts, feelings, behaviors, and body responses). If you employ unhealthy coping mechanisms to deal with stress, it might have a negative impact on your health. Stress's harmful consequences on your health can become a source of stress in and of itself. Just ask someone who is having trouble sleeping due to stress!

Is it possible for stress to be beneficial?

Mild stress may be beneficial and healthy when it comes to getting things done, addressing difficulties, improving drive, and being cautious. It aids a person's ability to adapt to and respond to their social and physical surroundings. This is referred to as "good stress." Extreme stress, on the other hand, can cause mental illnesses, strokes, ulcers, heart attacks, and other ailments.

Illness and stress

Your physical health is affected by your stress level and coping abilities. Stress levels that are too high might put you at risk for sickness. For example, if you are under a lot of stress, you are more likely to develop a cold or the flu. Stress has also been linked to the worsening of illnesses including rheumatoid arthritis, insulin-dependent diabetes, multiple sclerosis, and others. Chronic stress has a bad impact on your physical well-being as well. How you handle stress influences some of the linkages between stress and disease.

Stress Reduction

There is no one-size-fits-all approach to stress management. What is beneficial to one person may not be beneficial to another, and what is beneficial in one context may not be beneficial in another. The following are some of the most prevalent strategies for dealing with stress and staying healthy.

Concentrate on what you can do.

There is usually something you can do to handle stress in most circumstances.

Avoid the temptation to give up or run away from issues; while these coping strategies may feel nice in the short term, they can make stress worse in the long run.

Control your feelings.

When dealing with stress, it's natural to experience despair, rage, or fear.

- Talk about or write down your sentiments to try to communicate them. It will be more difficult to manage stress if you bottle up your feelings.

- Make an effort not to do harm to others. If you scream or cuss, you'll push them away when you need them the most.

- Many of the coping techniques outlined below might help you deal with your emotions.

Seek assistance.

Other people's social support is beneficial, especially if you feel you can't deal on your own. Support from family, friends, co-workers, and medical professionals can be invaluable.

Concentrate on concepts that are both useful and practical.

One of the most difficult aspects of managing with stress is this. It may appear impossible at times. However, if you concentrate on the bad, your stress level will rise, and you will lose drive to improve things.

Make a strategy of action.

Solving difficulties connected to components of a situation that you can control is one of the most effective strategies to reduce stress.

Break down a tough situation into small chunks.

Consider how you can best deal with the issue. You can choose to put aside other duties in order to focus on the major issue, or you can wait for the proper moment and location to act.

Self-care

Self-care can be tough to maintain during stressful times, but it can help you better manage challenges. The key to self-care is to find simple things you can do every day to make yourself feel better.

Here are some ideas for self-care activities. Consider what additional tasks you could do to assist you!

Take care of your relationships.

Your family, friends, and co-workers may be impacted by your stress, and they may also be contributing to the problem.

Instead of being hostile or quiet, be forceful about your demands. Being assertive implies expressing your requirements in a polite manner that allows you to consider both your own feelings and the feelings and needs of others.

Acceptance

There may be occasions when you are unable to make a change. This is often the most challenging component of stress management. Acceptance entails letting go of unpleasant sentiments and experiences without resisting or fighting them. It enables people to see and accept what they cannot change while concentrating on the steps they can take to better their life. All you can do at times is deal with your loss or unhappiness.

Overview

Module 1: What is Self-Compassion?

Module 2: Self-compassion preparations

Compassionate imagery is the third module.

Self-compassionate behaviors (module 4)

Module 1: What is Self-Compassion?

Introduction

To define self-compassion, we must first define compassion. They are, in fact, one and the same. Compassion is a state of mind that includes a collection of emotions, ideas, intentions, wants, drives, and behaviors that may be directed toward any sentient thing (i.e., ourselves, another person, a group of people, a society, animals, the environment, etc.). As a result, when we talk about self-compassion, we're referring to a mindset that is focused on ourselves.

Four important points are emphasized in various definitions:

1. be aware of your surroundings. The awareness or sensitivity to the knowledge that some form of 'suffering' is taking place. Suffering can refer to an excruciating battle with emotional, mental, or bodily anguish, or all three.

2. Bring everything back to normal. Recognize that this form of anguish is experienced by everyone. At some time in our lives, we all suffer pain in varied degrees. The fact that we are in pain is not a result of our own faults or failures; we are not to blame for it, and we are not alone in our suffering.

3. Generosity. Not avoiding or dismissing suffering, but instead responding to it with sentiments of love, caring, warmth, and concern.

4. A sense of relief. concentrating our efforts on alleviating the suffering, whether by further comfort and loving deeds, a useful viewpoint on the problem, or the strength and bravery to do other essential measures to address the problem

What is the significance of self-compassion?

Importance in Evolution

All animals, including humans, have evolved a strong urge to care for and be cared for. Being cared for from infancy is critical to our existence, and we cannot flourish without it. The ability to receive care and be motivated to offer care to others is critical to the human race's survival as a species. When this is done well, individuals collaborate, encourage one another, and prosper. Although receiving care from others is obviously vital, we now know that believing that we can only meet our need for care through other people is narrow-minded. It may also be quite beneficial in satisfying our desire for self-care and nurture.

Benefits to mental health and well-being

Self-compassion has been connected to our mental health and well-being, according to research. People who are more compassionate toward themselves have less mental health issues including sadness, anxiety, and stress, according to studies. These individuals also enjoy a higher quality of life, a stronger feeling of well-being, and fewer relationship issues. The hormone oxytocin, sometimes known as the "love hormone," is associated to compassion. This is a hormone that promotes bonding and intimacy and is therefore active during childbirth, physical affection, sex, when parents play with their children, when individuals play with their pets, and so on. Turning your compassion inward is known to induce the release of oxytocin and its accompanying soothing benefits. Essentially, self-compassion is linked to general life pleasure, which is something we can all achieve.

Bringing our emotions back into a healthy state

Because of the vital function it plays in regulating our emotions, self-compassion may provide us with a plethora of advantages. Paul Gilbert has written extensively on how three systems, the threat system, the drive system, and the calming system, influence our emotions, with each system playing a significant part in emotion regulation.

Threat: In order to live, all living creatures are skilled at predicting and avoiding hazards. We all have this defensive system ingrained into us. When you combine this with the human tendency to think a lot, you get the impression that the human mind has a default setting of seeking for terrible things, paying attention to them, and thinking about them again and over. As a result, our threat system is constantly active and working at full speed.

Our danger system is no longer activated by the appearance of a sabre-toothed tiger as it was in caveman times. Small imperfections or perceived inadequacies in our ability, looks, social skills, etc. are considered as dangers in today's culture. These things are viewed as a threat to our reputation, social standing, relationships, job, income, health, future, or happiness. As a result, for many of us, our danger system appears to be on high alert the majority of the time, constantly scanning for possible threats in order to keep us safe.

When the danger system is activated, emotional reactions such as fear, anger, and despair are triggered. These feelings serve to motivate us to defend ourselves. Fear drives us to recoil from danger, whereas sadness encourages us to cut ourselves off from danger. As a result, behavioral reactions like as "fight" (aggressive), "flight" (avoidance), or "freeze" are produced by the threat system (i.e., submissiveness or passivity).

When we are under a state of threat, our thinking becomes quite limited and pessimistic. In this situation, our mind does not appear to be able to quickly break free from its limited, negative concentration. When we are in danger mode, it is quite difficult to think in a balanced, logical, and sensible manner since it needs our brain to think in a complex manner. When our brain senses that we are in danger, it is not built to think critically. Sophisticated thinking requires time, which you don't have much of while you're in danger. Negative, narrow-minded thinking, on the other hand, moves quickly. This is crucial to understand because individuals frequently criticize their "illogical" thinking when they are experiencing distressing emotions, not knowing that their minds are meant to be irrational when they are in danger. The threat system is no longer a negative factor. It is important to remember that it is intended to protect us from actual threats (e.g., getting out of the way of a moving car). Many of our psychological issues, on the other hand, are caused by the threat system being activated too frequently when there is no genuine risk.

Drive: The drive system motivates us to attempt new things, to succeed, to create and achieve objectives, and to enjoy those exuberant "high-five moments" when we "win" something in life. The drive system motivates us to complete tasks and participate in daily activities. A drive system is beneficial since it allows us to progress in our lives. We would be lifeless and directionless if our drive system was not always active, which is an issue that may arise when we are sad.

The issue is that, like the threat system, this system may go into overdrive. This is especially true when we live in a competitive environment that constantly tells us that we must always accomplish more and be better, and that there is something wrong with us if we don't. We can immediately flip from the drive system to the threat system if we do not achieve our objectives, which is clearly not always doable. As a result, we may become stuck in an unhealthy cycle... When we encounter an obstacle, it's threat, threat, threat (e.g., "I need to achieve, achieve, accomplish"), and when we hit an obstacle, it's danger, threat, threat (e.g., "I need to achieve, achieve, achieve") (e.g., "I failed and so now a lot of bad things will happen to me").

Reassure: The calming system is a separate system that has a soothing effect on both the threat and drive systems, allowing them to relax when they are hyperactive. When we are just resting, feeling safe, quiet, and content, the soothing system is activated. You can't be in both danger and soothing mode at the same time, and you can't be in both driving and relaxing mode.

Kindness and loving experiences activate the calming mechanism. One approach to engage the calming system is to receive compassion from others, but self-compassion is also important. These modules are about locating that key and using it to regulate our emotions by engaging the calming system to quiet the threat and drive systems.

Why is it so difficult to be kind to oneself?

So, if self-criticism simply makes you feel worse, self-compassion is the way to go. But it isn't that easy. Compassionate treatment of oneself is challenging for most individuals. If this describes you, realize that you are not alone and that there might be a variety of causes.

Early life encounters

It is thought that some people's soothing systems are undeveloped as a result of receiving little attention, compassion, or care from others as children.

Compassionate encounters flourish and activate the calming system. It's difficult to learn what you haven't been taught.

So, if you didn't get much compassion from others as a child, it's reasonable that developing the ability to be compassionate toward oneself later in life will be more challenging.

The danger detection system

As previously stated, our brains are programmed to swiftly switch to danger mode in order to protect us.

Our default option is to see the negative. We overcome this attention bias, which does not come easily to us, when we focus on greater self-compassionate activities.

Lack of knowledge

Many of us aren't even conscious that we have issues or that we are treating ourselves in harmful critical ways. We can go through life doing what we've always done on autopilot. We become engrossed in our battle and fail to notice that we are struggling and that perhaps we might address it in the same manner that we could assist others with a comparable problem. We've never considered that treating oneself with kindness is a choice.

Self-compassion beliefs that are negative

Self-compassion may make some of us uncomfortable. Self-compassion is a concept that is rarely taught or discussed, and as a result, it might have a negative connotation. Some individuals believe that self-compassion is excessively "warm and fuzzy" and that it leads to sloth, self-absorption, or self-pity.

Self-criticism is the polar opposite of self-compassion.

Being sympathetic to oneself and so engaging the calming mechanism does not come easy to most individuals. Self-criticism, on the other hand, appears to be a lot easier to say than self-compassion. Self-criticism is a way of thinking in which we talk to ourselves in a negative, derogatory, and scolding manner. As a result, self-criticism can either activate the danger system directly or, if the threat system is already active for other reasons, the reaction through self-criticism can keep it alive.

The substance of self-critical thoughts can be harsh, and the tone can be frigid, harsh, and accusatory. It's as though we're reprimanding or rebuking ourselves in a harsh or severe manner. This way of thinking is prevalent in our culture and may be found in all of us to varied degrees. Most people will be labeled "dumb" or "idiot" if they commit a minor error. This is the gentler side of self-criticism. Others have a habit of speaking angrily to oneself, while others have a habit of hurling expletives at themselves. Because they believe they do not deserve to be treated better, some severe self-critics may experience feelings of self-hatred, self-loathing, or self-contempt.

Some frequent instances of self-critical remarks include the following:

You're a moron...I'm an idiot...you're worthless and pitiful... I'm completely hopeless... That is something you should not have done.... I'm not sure why I did it... you should've known better... I'm never going to get it right... You could just quit up now... there's no use in continuing...

You'll observe that some self-critics express themselves in the first person (I am...), while others do it in the second person (I am..). (you are...). You'll also observe that self-criticism is frequently linked to the following types of problematic thinking:

Making broad and disparaging remarks about ourselves based on our actions in a specific context is known as labeling.

Should: Using "should" phrases to impose unjustified obligations or pressure on oneself; and

Overgeneralize: assume that a negative example applies to all situations.

Ask yourself the following questions to become more aware of your own self-critical thinking style:

What are some of your common self-criticisms?

What do you say to/about yourself on a regular basis?

What's the best way to say these things? What is the tone of your inner voice? Is there someone who it reminds you of?

How does it make you feel when you criticize yourself?

What do you believe the negative implications of talking to oneself in this manner are?

Module 2: Self-Compassion Preparation

To be able to respond compassionately to ourselves, we must first recognize that we are struggling and recognize when our minds go into self-critical thinking, which just adds to our distress. We must also be able to slow down and avoid becoming engulfed in the whirlpool of our negative thoughts and sensations. We can't decide to attempt anything different unless we slow down and become more conscious... To adopt a more empathetic stance. All of the new self-compassion tactics you'll learn in the next courses will be meaningless unless you first slow down and notice what's going on inside of you. This module will assist you in developing these abilities. Slow breathing will be taught to assist you slow down your instinctive self-critical reactions and activate the calming system, which has a relaxing effect. You'll also learn to retrain your attention so that you're more aware of what your mind is doing and actively focus on what you want your mind to focus on, with compassion for yourself becoming a new focus of attention.

Taking it easy

When it comes to our bodily and mental well-being, breathing is crucial. Our sympathetic nervous system is activated when we are in threat mode. This system is in charge of getting our bodies 'revved up.' As a result, our respiratory rate may quicken, and we may experience a variety of other physiological changes as we prepare to fight, flee, or freeze. The prefrontal cortex (the portion of our brain responsible for intellect, logic, and decision-making) briefly shuts down to allow the more primitive section of our brain to recognize and respond to danger to take over (the amygdala).

Because our brains are distracted by the continual alert of danger, it is extremely difficult for us to think in a constructive, balanced, and self-compassionate manner under these conditions. So, what are our options? We must, however, take things more slowly. We need to activate the parasympathetic nervous system's opposing power. Our sympathetic nervous system is connected with danger mode, whereas our parasympathetic nervous system is involved with calming mode, which relaxes our body and mind. Our prefrontal brain has a chance to get back into gear in this calmer condition, allowing for more balanced and deliberate thinking. We have little chance of reacting to what's going on inside us with self-compassion without this soothing influence.

Slow down your breathing.

The key to slowing down the body and mind while also activating the parasympathetic nervous system is to breathe slowly. Slow breathing assists us in pressing the pause and restart buttons. Slow breathing may appear easy, but it's actually a remarkably effective approach for shifting from threat to soothing state.

10-14 breaths per minute is a typical breathing rate. Our respiration rate might be substantially greater than this when we are nervous or feel threatened. We advocate slowing down your breathing to roughly 5 breaths per minute with the breathing pace we prescribe, so we really slow things down.

Slowing down entails modifying your breathing method as well as slowing down your breathing rate. You'll be well on your way to activating the calming system and preparing yourself for the self-compassion tactics to come if you follow the instructions below.

Step 1: Make sure you're seated or resting in a comfy chair.

Step 2: Take a four-second inhale (through your nose if possible).

Step 3: Take a deep breath and hold it for 2 seconds.

Step 4: Hold your breath for 6 seconds before exhaling (again through the nose if possible).

Step 5: Hold your breath for a few seconds before inhaling again.

Step 6: Now it's time to practice, practice, practice!

Retrain your focus.

Another component that influences our emotional and physical well-being is where and how our mind concentrates its attention. We are usually unaware of what we are going through and rely on our ideas and feelings to get us through life. This is commonly referred to as "autopilot" or "mindlessness."

To cultivate self-compassion, we must first understand that we are struggling and that self-criticism is fueling our struggle.

We must also be able to mentally withdraw from what we are experiencing in order to examine what is going on in our thoughts and feelings rather than being overly involved with them. We need to retreat just enough to think about what's going on, but not enough to run away from our problem, just as a loving person would not run away from someone in pain.

Finally, in order to engage the calming system when needed, we must be able to intentionally change our attention to more self-compassionate ideas, which means we must choose where to focus our attention.

Taken together, this indicates we need to practice catching, observing, and redirecting our attention. We notice where our attention has been directed, examine it objectively, and then purposefully shift it to where we want it to be at that moment. Then, of course, repeat. Taking notes, watching, and redirecting as needed, since, as we all know, our attention wanders a lot!

So, how do we focus our attention to accomplish these three goals? We must, after all, exercise them on a regular basis! Consider your attention to be a muscle: if you don't train it on a regular basis, it will grow weak and less effective.

You may consistently train your attention in two ways: Both mindfulness-based techniques for retraining attention include focused on ordinary chores and meditation. Mindfulness is a word that refers to paying conscious attention to what is going on in the present moment while maintaining an accepting attitude about what you see. As a result, you become an observer of what you're going through (e.g., your breath, body sensations, thoughts, feelings, sounds, tastes, smells, sights, etc.). Don't categorize what you're going through as good or terrible. Don't try to modify or halt what you're going through. Simply keep an eye on things.

Mindfulness also entails learning to recognize when your attention has strayed from the current moment to anything else, and then gently bringing it back to the present moment. Mindfulness is not an attempt to control or eliminate your thoughts and feelings. Instead, it's about allowing them to exist within you while choosing to return your focus to something you want to focus on in the current now.

Concentrate on routine duties.

You may have observed that you are not truly focused on the work at hand when doing monotonous domestic duties like cleaning the dishes or ironing, but rather on autopilot. Focusing on a banal task entails progressively exercising and training your attention to focus on a mundane activity.

The advantage of concentrating on daily duties is that you won't have to do anything extra. It's simply a question of shifting how you focus your attention on the tasks you're already doing.

Make a list of the numerous normal actions you perform that you may utilize to improve your attention. Sitting, walking, eating, washing, and brushing your teeth are examples of everyday duties, not only housekeeping.

Try to be aware of all the sensory components of your jobs when executing them on a daily basis. Concentrate on the senses (touch, sight, hearing, smell, and taste) that are most relevant for the activity. Bring your attention back to the work whenever you find your mind drifting from the task, which occurs to everyone. Focus impartially on one or more of the following:

Feel: How does the action make you feel? What is the texture of the material (rough, smooth, etc.)? With which parts of your body are you in contact? Are there some parts of your body that come into contact with the work more than others?

What do you observe about the assignment while you're looking at it? What draws your attention? What does the job entail? What about the lighting, shadows, shapes, and colors?

What kinds of noises do you hear? What kinds of noises are connected to the task?

Smell: What odors do you detect? Do they alter their behavior during the task? How many different scents are there?

Taste: What flavors do you detect? Do they alter their behavior during the task? What is the flavor quality like?

Meditation

You may teach yourself to be more aware of what your attention is stuck on (particularly thoughts and feelings) by practicing meditation. You can also train yourself to divert your attention to a present topic of your choice and cope with your unavoidable digressive thoughts. Being conscious of your breathing and noticing when your attention wanders away from the breath, catch it, and bring it back to the breath as your anchor in the present now is a frequent meditation practice. Your breath is something that is constantly there yet that we are often unaware of. As a result, it's the ideal focus point for retraining your attention.

Steps to Meditation 1) Sit in a chair and adopt a comfortable position to begin the activity. What thoughts, feelings, and bodily sensations are you experiencing? Allow yourself to just identify, observe, and explain these feelings without passing judgment on them or attempting to modify or eradicate them. Complete this challenge in 30 seconds to 1 minute.

2) Now focus your attention on your breath, focusing on the sensations of inhaling and exhaling. From moment to moment, focus your attention on the back and forth flow of the feelings in your abdomen, letting go of thoughts with each exhale. With each breath, tell yourself to "relax" or "let go." If your attention wanders to other ideas, feelings, or sensations, don't try to modify or eliminate them. Simply take notice of them and let them occur. Then let go of your concentrate and return it to

your breath. This should take no more than 1 to 2 minutes.

3) Now shift your focus to feeling your entire body breathing and noticing the feelings all throughout your body. If you're experiencing intense emotions, tell yourself, "Whatever it is, it's OK, just let me experience it." Allow yourself to breathe with those sensations, and if your mind wanders to bothersome ideas or sensations, simply record them and let them go - then return your attention to feeling your whole-body breathing. Continue for another 1 to 2 minutes.

As you get more comfortable with this meditation, consider lengthening steps 2 and 3 until the meditation lasts 10 minutes or more. It's crucial to note that the purpose of attention training is frequently overlooked. Over time, practicing concentration on everyday tasks and meditation will: - Help you become more aware of where your attention is at any given moment, so you can recognize when it is fixated on pain, suffering, and self-criticism; - Help you flexibly shift your attention to where you'd like it to be - perhaps using some of the self-compassion strategies to come; and - Help you notice when your attention inevitably wanders away from self-compassion, and be able to bring it back; and

It's also crucial to remember that the purpose of focusing on daily duties and meditation isn't to have flawless, continuous concentration in the present moment all of the time, or to have an empty mind with no thoughts or sensations. That is unthinkable! If you try to concentrate on the current moment, you will notice that your mind wanders. You may begin to reflect on the future or the past, or you may become self-critical, or something else may draw your focus. That's OK. That is what the mind is capable of. The goal is to become aware of when your mind wanders off track and gently bring it back to the current "job" (i.e., whatever you have been focusing on - the breath, laundry, brushing your teeth, etc.). The goal is to become aware of your attention, to detect and observe where it is, and to bring it back to the present as needed.

Avoid criticizing yourself if you detect your thoughts straying throughout these attention retraining activities. Rather, attempt to summon some sympathy. This is, after all, entirely natural. Instead, see each "digression" as a chance to practice refocusing your attention on the present moment. Consider it this way: the skill you're learning isn't how to keep perfect attention, but rather how to catch it when it wanders and bring it back. So it doesn't matter how frequently your attention wanders; it's an important element of the training.

Module 3: Compassionate Imagery

According to studies, images may be quite effective at eliciting emotions. Our brain isn't particularly excellent at telling the difference between a picture and reality. As a result, it will frequently analyze and respond to a picture as if it were genuine. Consider a meal that you truly enjoy... in my case, it would be chocolate cake!

Now close your eyes and pretend that you are eating this cuisine. Consider going close to it and smelling it... what do you notice? What is your current state of mind... do you have any bodily feelings... how does your mouth feel?

Many people experience a bodily sensation when they visualize the meal they want, and their mouths may even start to drool! This is due to the fact that our brain is processing and reacting to the visual as if the meal were there in front of us.

But what does self-compassion have to do with thoughts of chocolate cake? We must first create compassionate sentiments in order to build self-compassion, and then focus those feelings toward ourselves when we are facing issues. If we know that visuals are a powerful tool for evoking emotions, we should put that information to good use. So, when we come across an image that makes us feel sympathetic, we may utilize it to turn our compassion toward ourselves.

Our objective is to create an image that instills in us a compassionate mindset, causing us to feel, think, and act compassionately. We'll now look at two different sorts of compassionate pictures that you could find useful. We recommend that you experiment with both photos to find which one best elicits sentiments of compassion in you.

Creating the ideal compassion picture

Relationships are tricky, and some of us may not have individuals in our life with whom we feel pure compassion, making the picture exercise we just described difficult for them to genuinely benefit from. If this is the case, the prior image will not evoke complete, unadulterated compassion, which is exactly what we want.

As a result, we frequently find this practice to be more beneficial, because it allows you to imagine your own ultimate vision of compassion. This compassion fantasy picture may be anything you want it to be. When it comes to establishing your own distinctive image that expresses pure compassion, there are no right or wrong answers. In truth, the image you create is unimportant. It makes no difference if the image is fantastical or realistic. Remember, we're simply using this picture to elicit pure compassion in ourselves, so any image that does this is OK.

As you are well aware, begin by shutting your eyes and slowing your breathing...

Do you notice what pictures, emotions, or feelings come to mind when you think about compassion right now? Don't push yourself too hard; just accept what is, or let things come and go as they will...

Allow an image to develop in your mind that represents compassion to you. Take the time to create a picture that represents all of the aspects of compassion. It's fine if nothing comes to mind right away. Simply take your time and observe what appears, no matter how bizarre it may appear. It doesn't have to be a vivid visual; a sense of the image is also acceptable. It's acceptable if numerous photos appear (similar to a slide show), and we'll see which one you choose over time.

Try to create a mental image that makes you feel good...

Allow for an image that expresses empathy for you, your problems, and your emotions...

Allow yourself to be surrounded with images of love, care, and concern for your well-being...

Allow yourself to be surrounded by a powerful, smart, and supportive image... Allow yourself to be seen in a way that embraces you for who you are...

Now consider if the image depicts a person, something actual or imagined, an animal, another entity, or a natural phenomenon. Is it a child or an adult? Is it a man or a woman? What colors or types of light do you connect with it? What emotions does this image evoke in you? What bodily sensations do such sentiments elicit in your body? What is the look on your face in the image? What message does it provide you through its posture or stature? What does it sound like or how does it convey to you? What does it convey to you? What is the tone of the voice? What exactly is it doing to assist or console you?

You can let go of the vision and open your eyes when you're ready.

Now, in words and/or images, explain your ultimate caring image.

(Describe it in words and/or draw a picture) is my ideal compassionate image.

____

____

Self-compassionate behaviors (module 4)

Taking care of ourself

The most apparent self-compassionate behavior that comes to mind is being nice and caring to yourself in the way you treat yourself and how you spend your time. Taking care of oneself on a daily basis might act as a prophylactic or buffer when we are experiencing emotional distress. Doing something nice for oneself, especially when we're down, may help us cope with and overcome tough emotional situations, just as we would attempt to help a friend in need.

Self-soothing or self-care is a term used to describe how we take care of ourselves by carefully selecting the activities we engage in. Self-soothing typically entails intentionally engaging in activities that make us feel safe and loved while also assisting us in getting through unpleasant situations.

What people find self-soothing varies tremendously. What one person considers to be adequate self-care may be a nightmare for another. Experiment with different hobbies to see what feels nice and what makes you feel like you're looking after yourself and being kind to yourself. A list of suggested self-soothing activities is on the next page. The idea is that you don't have to participate in every activity on the list, but that you may pick and choose the ones you want to do. A detailed list can also assist you in identifying more self-soothing activities that may be beneficial to you.

Examine the list and make a note of the things you'd want to do the next time you're in difficulties. Other activities that spring to mind can be written in the space given. The purpose of these activities is to explore what occurs when you decide to be nice to yourself by engaging in self-soothing activities, rather than to alleviate your emotional suffering or fix the problem.

SELF- SOOTHING ACTIVITIES:

Make yourself a nice meal or snack.   Go out to have a nice meal or snack

Have a picnic   Meet up with a friend

Call a friend   Take a walk in beautiful surroundings

Look at beautiful art or scenery   Visit a beautiful place

Enjoy time at the beach   Put on soothing music

Enjoy the sounds of nature   Take a bubble bath Have a massage

Do your nails   Read a good book

Watch a good movie or series TV   Pet your dog or cat

Hug yourself Meditate   Breathe slowly

Take a break

Summary

- ❖ To cultivate self-compassion, we must first be able to slow down, engage the parasympathetic nervous system, and activate our soothing mode. To attain this soothing condition, we employ steady breathing, which puts us in the greatest possible position to think and behave compassionately toward ourselves.

- ❖ We learn to become aware of where our attention is by doing exercises in concentrating on ordinary tasks and meditation, gently directing it to a specific present task, and capturing and returning it to the present task when it wanders.

- ❖ When it comes to self-compassion, taking care of oneself by engaging in self-soothing activities is a top priority. Self-soothing entails engaging in nurturing activities that make us feel safe and loved, as well as activities that can help us get through stressful situations. It's critical that we schedule these activities into our week on a regular basis and that we have particular activities in mind for when we're feeling down.

Bonus Chapter
Mindfulness

Mindfulness activities help people understand themselves as a process in a more positive light. Floating Leaves on a Moving Stream is a good closed-eye practice (ibid.). Subjects imagine themselves bending over at the brink of a stream, observing the leaves drifting by. The patient is asked to visualize each idea being placed on a floating leaf. When he detects that one of the ideas is luring him away from the work of placing the thoughts on the leaves, he pushes himself to return to it. The therapist inquires if the client's ideas appear to be flowing like water. Other pictures, such as automobiles going by on a road, might be used for this activity.

Imagine clouds separating in the sky as an alternative to this practice. The patient imagines himself resting in a verdant field, gazing up into the sky. He imagines that his experience is dedicated to a phrase or picture associated with one of the clouds. The therapist next asks the patient to visualize each idea being assigned to a cloud. When the client's mind wander, he should yank his devotion back to the skies.

Here are some anxiety-relieving mindfulness exercises:

1. take a deep breath

Allow the air to flow over your entire body by breathing in through your nose and out through your mouth in seven-second repetitions. Let go of all ideas while you breathe. Also, be aware of how the air is infusing your body with vitality by paying attention to your breath. Allow your awareness to go through your body, out through your mouth and nostrils, and into the energy surrounding you.

2. Observation

Pick an unremarkable thing in your local vicinity and observe it for a minute or two to connect with the beauty of the natural environment. Do nothing except pay attention to it. Relax. Perceive the thing as if you've never seen it before, and pay attention to every detail. Make a connection with this object's life force.

3. a state of thought

Consider a simple and seemingly inconsequential activity you perform on a daily basis, such as opening a door. Begin by observing all of the minute nuances of your motions and sensations. When you open a door, for example, place your hand on the doorknob and pay attention to how you feel and where the entry goes. Pay attention to the things that come to mind while you carry out this simple task.

Make a mental note of any unwelcome thoughts and then let them go. When you're doing something repetitious, you might also consider your standards. Appreciate food when you smell it, for example. Consider the opportunity to share meals with family and friends.

4. pay attention

The purpose of this exercise is to bring your attention back to the current moment while softening the effect of your previous experiences and preconceptions. To decrease the intrusion of bad memories and the related uneasiness or anguish, focus on the current moment.

Pick a piece of music that you haven't heard before. Make an effort to listen with an open mind. Close your eyes and put on headphones. Pay attention to how the music changes, then dissect and explore each variety of sound. Consider the timbre, location, and tones of each voice if there are lyrics. Allow your thoughts to meld with the sound by listening deliberately and carefully. Set aside your prejudices and simply listen.

5. immerse yourself

This is a meditation activity to help you relax. Allow the strength of your daily errands and aspirations to fade away. Be satisfied with what you have right now. Choose one action, such as doing the dishes, and pay attention to every aspect. Consider it as a whole new experience, and take note of everything.

Embrace the activity, the sensations, and the motions. Recognize the novelty in routine work. To engage yourself in the exercise and tune into what is repeating - intellectually, physically, and spiritually - be conscious of every movement.

6. admiration

Pay attention to five items or individuals in your everyday life that you don't typically cherish sufficiently. Appreciate the mundane, the simple yet significant details that make up our lives. Other individuals may be present, as well as items such as faucets and power wires, plants, walkways, and delivery vehicles.

A compassionate body scan

Please lie down on your back with your hands approximately six inches from your sides and your feet about shoulder-width apart in a comfortable posture. Place one or two hands over your heart (or another relaxing location) as a reminder to maintain compassionate awareness throughout the practice. Feel your hands' warmth and delicate touch. Return your arms to your sides after three deep, relaxing breaths.

If you have negative feelings or connections with a certain body area, or if you are in pain, you might want to lay your hand on that part of your body as a gesture of love, possibly envisioning warmth and kindness pouring through your hand and into your body.

If a region of your body becomes too tough to stay with, gradually move on to another body part for the time being, making this practice as soft and calm as possible.

Beginning with your left foot's toes, we'll see whether there are any feelings In your toes. Do your toes feel hot or cold, dry or wet? Simply sensing your toes' sensations - ease, agony, or nothing at all - and allowing each experience to be exactly as it is.

Then go on to your left foot's soles. Are there any feelings there? Despite the fact that your feet have such a little surface area, they support your entire body all day. They put forth so much effort. Now, if only for a brief while, we're expressing our gratitude to them.

If there is any discomfort, release any tension and let that place to relax as if it were covered in a warm blanket you enjoy, addressing feeling with compassionate words like "There's a little soreness there, it's alright for now."

Feel your entire foot now. If your feet are in decent shape today, you may be grateful for the lack of discomfort.

Moving your focus up your leg, one component at a time, observing any bodily sensations, enjoying if the area feels good and offering love if it hurts. Slowly, staying on the left side, make your way to your...

o The Ankle

o Calf and shin

o Kneeling

When you discover your mind has strayed, as it will, just redirect your attention to the feelings in the specific portion of your body.

If you're worried or critical about a certain body part, lay your palm over your heart and softly breathe, or place your hand directly on the body area.

You might also say something kind like, "May my [knees] be at peace." "May they be well," you say, and then restore your focus to the basic feelings that arise.

Loving-Kindness Meditation

This is more of a pen-and-paper exercise than a casual activity that can be used in everyday life. The goal of the activity is to help you come up with loving-kindness and compassion words that are significant to you. If you currently have phrases and want to keep using them, attempt this activity as an experiment, but don't feel obligated to come up with new ones.

To begin, close your eyes, place your palm over your heart or anywhere else on your body, and slowly breathe.

What do I require?

* *Take a minute to let your heart to open gradually. You may envision your heart opening out to itself, like a flower in the light.*

* *After that, ask yourself, "What do I require?" What exactly do I require?*

Your day is not complete if this requirement has not been met on a particular day.

Allow the response to be a common human need, such as a desire to be connected, compassionate, peaceful, and free.

Allow yourself time to come up with one or more words on your own.

* *When you're ready, open your eyes and write down what you genuinely need as a person.*

• *If you choose, you might turn your wants into self-wishes, such as "May I feel connected to others."*

"May I be gentle to myself," says the narrator.

"May I live in peace," says the narrator.

o "May I be at liberty"

You can also use the word or words exactly as they came to mind.

What Do I Wish I Could Hear?

• *Now close your eyes and ask yourself the following questions:*

"Can you tell me what I'd want to hear from others?"

"What are the words that I yearn to hear addressed to me because, as a human, I really need to hear them?"

"If I could, what words would I like to have whispered into my ear every day for the rest of my life, words that would make me grateful every time I hear them?" 'Oh, thank you...thank you...thank you,' I'd think on the inside."

Wait for words to enter through the entrance of your heart. Have faith in yourself. Listen.

• *Gently open your eyes again, and spend a few moments to jot down what you've heard. If you heard a lot of words, try condensing them into a single phrase—a message to yourself.*

• *Words we yearn to hear from others are frequently traits we wish to embody in our own lives or attitudes we want to be certain of. It's a series of subliminal wishes for ourselves. Longing to hear "I love you," for example, indicates that we want to know that we are lovable.*

Self-Compassion Script

When you're experiencing stress or mental distress, try to locate the source of the discomfort in your body. What part of your body is the most affected? Make touch with your body's sensations as they emerge.

Slowly repeat to yourself:

1. "This is a difficult time."

That is what mindfulness is all about. Other possibilities include:

" I'm in pain.

" Oh no!

" This is a difficult situation.

2. "Suffering is an unavoidable aspect of existence."

That is common humanity; other possibilities are:

• I'm not alone; there are others who feel the same way I do.

• We all face challenges in our life.

• This is how it feels when someone is going through a difficult time.

Place your hands over your heart, or wherever you find it relaxing, and enjoy the warmth and soft touch of your hands.

To yourself, say:

3. "May I be kind to myself," or "May I give myself what I need," is another way of putting it.

In moments like this, see if you can come up with terms for what you're looking for.

- *Is it possible for me to accept myself as I am?*

- *May I come to accept myself for who I am.*

- *May I be forgiven?*

- *May I be courageous.*

- *Could you please be patient with me?*

- *May I enjoy a life filled with love*

If you're having trouble finding the proper words, imagine that a close friend or loved one is facing the same difficulties as you: what would you say to them? If your buddy could only speak a few words, what would they be? What message would you wish to give, heart to heart?

Now check if you can send yourself the same message.

Self-compassion and compassion for others script

- *Please take three deep, calming breaths while sitting in a comfortable posture.*

- *Tune in to the noises around you, bringing yourself into the present moment by just listening to whatever comes to your ears.*

- *Locate your body in the room and note your posture as if you were looking in the mirror.*

- *Next, move your consciousness within your body, noting the universe of sensations that are occurring there right now—sitting in the middle of your body's pulsation and vibration, just as you did with sound.*

- *Place a hand over your heart or wherever and experience the warmth and soft touch of your hand to enhance the purpose of bringing loving-kindness to your consciousness.*

- *Begin by giving yourself a deep breath, a smile, or a remark like the one below to express a heartfelt wish for oneself:*

May I have a joyful and pain-free life.

- *When you're ready, allow yourself to be aware of any humans or other living beings who come into your consciousness, and give them something positive, such as a breath, a smile, or the words:*

May you have a joyful and pain-free life.

- *Spend as much time as you like with this creature, expressing well wishes, and then wait for the next one to come in your head; take your time.*

• And, at any point, returning to yourself, especially if you need to ground your awareness in your own body or soothe yourself.

• Let go of the meditation now and accept yourself precisely as you are in this moment.

• Slowly open your eyes.

Friend with Compassion

Please sit or lie down in a comfortable position, close your eyes gently, and take a few deep breaths to relax into your body. Place one or two hands over your heart or another calming location to remind yourself to give yourself loving care.

• Visualize yourself in a safe and comfortable place—it could be a warm room with a fireplace burning, a peaceful beach with warm sun and a cool breeze, or a forest glade; it could also be an imaginary place, such as floating on clouds...anywhere you might feel peaceful and safe. Allow yourself to linger in this place and enjoy the feeling of comfort (pause).

• A warm and sympathetic presence—a caring friend—an ideal figure who exemplifies the attributes of knowledge, strength, and unconditional love—will soon pay you a visit.

• This being may be a spiritual figure, a knowledgeable, compassionate instructor, someone from your history who fully represents the attributes of love and wisdom

(perhaps a beloved grandfather), or it could appear in your mind for the first time right now.

• Furthermore, your caring companion may take on no physical shape at all, preferring to be a loving presence or a brilliant light.

• Your caring buddy genuinely cares about you and want for you to be happy and at peace.

• Allow such a creature to appear in your thoughts, visualizing this being—this presence—in as much detail as possible (long pause)

• You have the option to leave your safe spot and meet your compassionate friend, or to invite him or her in. (pause) If you choose, please do so immediately.

• Getting into the correct position in regard to your compassionate friend—whatever seems right—maybe near, maybe at a respectful distance.

• Then, with nothing to do except absorb the moment, let yourself to feel what it's like to be in the company of this individual (pause).

• Allowing yourself to absorb in the unconditional love and compassion that this being has for you; if you can't, that's good, too...this being feels it all the same.

Guided Meditation for Anxiety, Sleep, and Other Issues in 10 Minutes

You may have observed that the mind may be rather loud by now.

And you could be concerned that you aren't doing everything correctly.

Because you can't stop all of your thoughts, meditation might not be for you.

But that is precisely what meditation is meant to be.

We're merely paying attention to our thoughts, seeing how they come and go.

And paying attention strengthens our attention muscle because each time we notice ourselves having a thought and bring ourselves back, we increase that muscle.

It's like folding a sheet of paper: it requires focus and effort the first time you do it, but it gets simpler with practice.

So, be nice with yourself and try if you can observe yourself with a sense of amusement and wonder.

Observing your approach to something new.

Are you becoming irritated, or are you being patient with yourself?

But for the time being, let's get started.

As we did throughout our first week.

You can select a comfy seat and close your eyes when you're ready.

I want you to pay attention to your thoughts today as you sit down.

'Just as you take your seat.' Take note of what appears.

Are you pondering what happened before you sat down, or what has to be accomplished later in the day?

Just take note of the notion.

Now take three cleaning breaths in through your nose and out through your mouth.

As though you were constantly totally and thoroughly aware of your breath.

Breathe deeply into your chest and belly.

And if a thought arises, simply restore your attention to the feeling of your breath, noticing where you are breathing.

The air fills your lungs like balloons in a three-dimensional breath when it meets your nose.

You can now resume your normal breathing pattern of inhaling and exhaling via your nose.

Guided Meditation for body scan in 10 Minutes

Taking the time to check in with your surroundings as normal.

First, take note of any sounds that surround you.

Noises from the street, the hum of the ventilation system

You could even start to hear the sound of your own breath.

Feeling yourself in your surroundings now

Being totally present and noticing oneself if a thought arises

Observing your position in the chair

Where your feet come into contact with the ground

Maybe it's the feeling of the air on your skin.

And, as is customary, begin scanning your physique.

Simply return to the body scan when you detect ideas coming in.

So let's start with the soles of our feet, calves, and thighs.

Keeping in mind to scan your joints, as well as each body part

Observing if you are scanning with your body in mind or merely thinking about it.

I'm concentrating on tuning in to the sensations of the body scan.

And, as always, paying attention to whether or not you are experiencing any emotions in your body

Maybe you have stiffness in your shoulders and jaw.

And simply observing the sensations in your body without passing judgment

When you observe a thought returning to where you left off in the body, repeat the process.

And now we're going to start repeating our slogan.

On your inhale, silently repeat "breathing in" to yourself.

"Breathing out" occurs when you exhale.

Easily, without effort

20 seconds

And when you sense your mind wandering, gently bring it back to your chant, remembering that this is the practice.

Taking a Deep Breath

Taking a breath out

20 seconds

And if you sense your thoughts drifting, simply catch yourself and bring it back to your breath.

Inhaling deeply

Taking a breath out

15 seconds

Now it's only a matter of letting your mind wander.

Increasing your understanding

As though you're in the middle of a movie

Just realizing how far back you can zoom out is enlightening.

25Sec

Now it's time to return our attention to our bodies.

Getting a feel for the chair's seat

Observing the air temperature on our skin

Any noises you hear

You can then open your eyes when you're ready.

So, today, before you leap, consider the following:

Take note of where your thoughts are leading you.

Are you looking forward to what you'll do next?

So check if you can make an effort to be more mindful of what's coming up next.

I'm attempting to be as present as possible.

And we'll see you tomorrow to find out how to cope with the remainder of the obstacles that you could encounter in your meditation practice.

Body scan in 20 Minutes

When you're ready, take a seat and close your eyes.

Keep in mind how little effort it takes to keep your eyes shut.

Are you attempting to maintain a specific position with your mouth?

See what happens if you simply relax your mouth and jaw naturally without exerting any effort.

Take note of how it settles into its ideal position.

Not clinched tightly, nor wide open.

Let's start with some slow, deep breathes.

In and out through the nose and mouth

On each in-breath, completely fill your lungs and belly.

With each out-breath, I'm emptying my lungs.

Repeat this process a couple more times.

Let's get back to your normal breathing on your next out-breath,

Through the nose, in and out.

Breathing without exerting any effort.

Allowing yourself to let go of the desire to regulate your breathing pattern.

Let's check in on what's going on in and around us while continuing to breathe.

Any noises can be heard.

Feel your body in your seat now.

Your feet are planted on the earth.

In your lap, your hands

Begin scanning your body from your feet to the crown of your head, tuning into your body.

Take your time with this.

Any feelings that may arise along the route should be felt.

As you scan upwards, simply bring awareness to the various regions of your body.

Feeling any sensations without putting a positive or negative name on them

If your focus wanders while you're doing this, gently bring it back to where you left off.

Take a moment to consider your current mood.

Detecting any powerful emotions you may be experiencing

Can you pinpoint where you're experiencing emotions in your body?

Perhaps your stomach,

Your sternum,

or the inside of your head

Emotions may be sensed throughout the body.

As usual, I'm only observing and not passing judgment on what's going on.

Now concentrate on your breathing.

Begin reciting your mantra while breathing in and out through your nose.

"Breathing in" on the inhale

"Breathing out" means exhaling.

Let's take a moment to breathe together for a minute or two.

We concentrate our concentration on the tip of our nose while repeating our chant.

(pause for 20 seconds)

Taking a deep breath

I'm exhaling.

If you find yourself losing focus, simply return to your breath and your mantra.

Taking a deep breath

Breathing Exhaustion

(pause for 20 seconds)

Whenever you notice yourself slipping into thought, catch yourself.

and gradually refocus your attention

It's the same as training a dog.

Over and over, with care and compassion, I've been leading it back.

(pause for 20 seconds)

Taking a deep breath

Breathing Exhaustion

(15 seconds of silence)

Allow the phrase to fade away and continue to breathe normally.

Transition now from a strict focus on your breath to just letting your mind wander.

Extending your awareness as far and wide as you can

Try to become aware of as many of your senses as possible.

Your body's weight on the seat

The noises that surround you

Observe your breathing.

Thinking

You will be guided by my voice.

See if you can mentally take a step back from everything.

And simply be conscious of what's going on.

without becoming engrossed in it

As if you were a moviegoer viewing a film

(15 seconds of silence)

Now, let's return to the body.

Returning to the sensation of inhaling and exhaling

The way your body interacts with the seat.

Your feet are firmly planted on the earth.

You've had your hands in your lap.

Now pay attention to the sounds around you.

Take a long, cleansing breath.

If you like, you can breathe out loudly.

Slowly open your eyes when you hear the bell.

So, how did your day go today?

Do you notice that you can more quickly catch yourself thinking the thoughts?

Script for Relaxation

Let's rest your body and mind for a few minutes.

Begin with a few slow, deep breaths, breathing all the way down into your stomach each time. Breathe in slowly through your nose, and feel your abdomen and lungs expand with air. Allow your breath to flow back out through your mouth, releasing any tension or stress you may have been holding on to.

Try it now: gently inhale a deep breath. Don't hurry it; simply gradually fill your lungs and belly with air, and when they're full, exhale fully. You'll notice that you're beginning to relax; your breath will dissolve tension as effortlessly as warm water melts ice.

Breathe in again, feeling your body fill with air...and when you're ready, release the breath, allowing it to flow out naturally until your lungs are empty. Let's take a third and final breath, nice and deep. Feel yourself relaxing as you gently release the breath.

As I describe each body part, I want you to bring your consciousness to it and relax it as completely as you can. You don't need to concentrate intensively on this job; simply feel or imagine a sense of relaxation and comfort going through each part of your body.

Allow your jaw muscles to loosen and let go. It's extremely usual for individuals to store a lot of tension in their jaw muscles, so start there. Pay attention to your jaw for a moment. There are a lot of really powerful muscles in that area. Just mentally connect with this part of your body and relax it.

Allow your eye muscles to relax, and your cheeks and forehead to relax. Allow this tranquil sensation to run down your neck, comfort your throat, and eliminate any tension as it gently glides down to your shoulders.

Allow your shoulders to soften, let go, and release all tension by giving them a moment of your attention and mentally repeating the word "relax."

Bring your consciousness to your arms now, and feel and envision them becoming free and limp, relaxed and at ease, all the way from your shoulders to the tips of your fingers.

Now bring your consciousness to your back muscles...all those muscles around your spine...just relax and let go. Now bring your awareness to your chest muscles...all those muscles surrounding your rib cage...send a mental note to this part of your body...relax.

Feel your stomach gradually rise and fall as you breathe in and out; let it soften and relax with each breath, releasing tension as each moment passes; you may feel yourself progressively drifting into a state of profound relaxation.

Now turn your attention to your thighs, and imagine all of those powerful supporting muscles relaxing and unwinding.

Allow your knees, calves, and feet to all relax.

Passive relaxation

This script was created to help you relax your mind and body completely. It's a great way to warm up before a guided meditation and just takes 7-9 minutes to read aloud.

If you read it slowly and gently, everyone within hearing will rapidly find themselves in an extremely peaceful frame of mind.

Find a quiet spot to sit and relax. Dim the lights and turn off your phone. This is your chance to shine. This is a moment for complete rest and inner peace.

Take a time to check if you're warm enough and that you're sitting comfortably. Place your hands in your lap loosely. Close your eyes now.

Inhale deeply for a long time, hold it for a bit, and then slowly exhale. Allow any tension to dissipate as you breathe in and out more deeply with each breath.

Take another long, slow, deep breath in, hold it for a few moments, and then exhale. With your out-breath, thoroughly empty your lungs.

Inhale deeply for a third time. Please take your time. Hold it for a few moments before releasing it. You may feel yourself slipping into a profound state of relaxation already.

As you raise your consciousness to the top of your head, continue to breathe slowly and softly. Feel the muscles in your forehead and temples relax as you perceive or imagine a sensation of calm spreading down from the top of your head.

Allow the muscles in your eyes to relax. Allow your cheeks and jaw to relax and release any tension.

Allow this serene sensation to run down your neck. It will loosen every muscle and fibre in your body.

This calming sensation deepens and warms with each breath you take. It penetrates deep into your shoulder muscles, relaxing and releasing them.

This serene sensation cascades down your shoulders and into your arms. It relaxes and soothes the muscles in your upper arms, forearms, and hands, all the way down to the tips of your fingers.

Your mind relaxes as your body relaxes, and your thoughts appear to lighten. You're sinking deeper and deeper into a dreamy state of calm and serenity.

Bring your attention to your chest and stomach now. As you breathe, notice how this part of your body rises and lowers gently. The pleasant feeling spreads throughout this area of your body, relaxing every muscle and organ. You can feel every single atom of stress being released.

Concentrate your attention on your upper back, and let this soothing sensation to spread down your spine. Feel every muscle in your back relax and unwind as it works its way down your body.

Your entire upper body appears to be loose, limp, and relaxed.

Allow yourself to get carried away by this peaceful feeling. With each breath, relax deeper and deeper.

Feel your hips relax as the serene sensation spreads throughout your lower body. Relax your buttocks, your thighs' backs, and your thighs' fronts. With each passing instant, feel all of these enormous, powerful muscular groups loosen and relax.

Relaxing sensations run down your knees and into your calves. Relax your ankles. Your feet can now unwind. Allow your entire lower body to relax fully, and let any lingering tension drain out via the tips of your toes.

You're at ease, tranquil, and unwinded.

Script for Rapid Relaxation

Locate a peaceful area where you can unwind. Allow your hands to fall naturally into your lap or by your side. Close your eyes now.

Inhale deeply and slowly via your nose, all the way down to your stomach. Hold your breath for a few seconds before exhaling through your mouth. As the air flows out of your lungs, let your breath to carry away all worry and anxiety.

Inhale slowly through your nose once again. Completely fill your lungs. Hold it for a few moments...then exhale through your lips. With your out-breath, thoroughly empty your lungs.

Feel as if the tension in your body is starting to dissipate.

Inhale deeply for a third time. Hold it for a few moments before releasing it.

With each breath, feel yourself relaxing further and deeper.

Bring your attention to your toes and feet. Inhale deeply through your nose, gently curling your toes down and tenseing the muscles in the soles of your feet as you do so. Hold your breath for a few seconds before letting go of the muscles in your feet as you exhale.

Bring your attention to your calf muscles now. Inhale deeply and tense your muscles by pointing your toes up towards your knees. Hold for a few seconds before letting those muscles relax as you exhale.

Now take a big breath in and tension your thigh muscles. Hold for a brief period before releasing all of your muscles. Concentrate on allowing them to become slack and loose.

Take a big breath in and tighten the muscles in your buttocks gradually. Hold the contraction for a few seconds before letting go of the breath. Feel the tightness in your muscles dissipate. Feel them fully unwind.

Take a big breath in and then contract your tummy muscles. Hold your breath for a second. Now take a deep breath and relax your muscles.

Pay attention to the muscles in your back. Arc your back slightly and tense these muscles while you gently breathe in.... Now exhale slowly and let your muscles to relax.

As you inhale deeply, pull your shoulders up towards your ears and clench these muscles. Now take a deep breath out entirely. Allow your tense muscles to relax and become limp.

Feel the weight in your body right now. Enjoy the sensation. Inhale deeply once again. Tighten all of the muscles in your arms by clenching your fists. Squeeze your muscles while holding your breath...then slowly relax and exhale. Allow your arms and hands to relax and become limp.

Squeeze your eyes shut and press your lips together to tighten the muscles in your face. Take a deep breath in. Hold for a moment...then exhale deeply and relax all of your face muscles. Feel your face become softer.

Inhale deeply and then open your mouth as wide as possible. Feel the muscles in your jaw expanding and tightening. Allow your mouth to softly shut as you exhale.

Take one last long breath in, totally filling your lungs...hold for a second, then release and relax. Allow every last molecule of stress to be carried away by the breeze.

From the tips of your toes to the top of your head, you are entirely calm. Enjoy this sensation as long as you want. Take your time, and then open your eyes when you're ready.

Positive Energy Meditation

Please take a comfortable sitting position where you will not be disturbed to begin.

If it feels wonderful to you, I'll now ask you to close your eyes.

Take a minute to feel your entire body in the place it's in, from the top of your head to the soles of your feet, and all the way down your spine to your sit bones.

Take a big breath in through your nose now. Hold your breath for a second. Exhale completely through your mouth.

Inhale deeply once again. Hold your breath for a second. Also, completely exhale. Allowing yourself to mentally let go of everything that is no longer benefitting you.

Last but not least. Inhale. Hold your breath for a second. And then totally exhale.

Allow your breathing to return to its natural rhythm, and just begin to notice how your body rises and falls as you inhale and exhale.

Take both hands to the center of your chest, where your heart is located, and repeat the mantra after me. I am sufficient.

Take this minute, whatever is going on in your life at the moment, wherever you are, to just be with whatever thoughts, feelings, and sensations occur without judgement.

Please say it again: "I am enough."

Now expand your consciousness to the top of your head, then up above you, and begin to visualize a light or energy source above your head. It might be a golden or white light, or even a liquid light falling from the sky and into your mind.

Visualize a beam of light entering your head, neck, and shoulders. Allow the light to penetrate your arms, hands, and entire torso. Feel the light going down your legs and into your feet as it descends to your hips.

Start to awaken the experience of lightness throughout your entire body by becoming aware of your entire body as a source of light.

Recite the slogan "I am enough" many times.

Visualize roots connecting and grounding you to the soil by connecting to any portions of your body that contact the ground beneath you – your sit bones and maybe the soles of your feet. Now send your mind all the way down to the earth's core, and begin seeing another light source.

Allow this light from the earth's core to flow up into the soles of your feet, your legs, and your hips. Allow this calming light to enter your body, hands, and arms. Allow this light to enter your shoulders, neck, and entire head.

Consider your entire body to be a shining source of light. Extend this light about you to create a protective aura that wraps around your entire body like a cocoon of brilliant light.

I am enough, repeat after me.

If there's anything in your life right now that isn't benefiting you, see it as grey smoke exiting your body. Allow the protecting aura of light to turn the grey energy into bright shining light.

Consider everything to be in a perpetual state of flux and transformation.

Allow yourself to relax in your soft cocoon without condemning yourself. Allow yourself to be present in whatever situation happens.

(Give yourself some breathing room – 1-2 minutes)

Recite the slogan "I am enough" many times.

Regain awareness of your body's natural rise and fall when you inhale and exhale.

From the top of your skull to your sit bones and soles of your feet, feel your entire physical body in the area it occupies.

Visualize this glowing aura or cocoon of light enveloping and protecting you in the future if you ever feel low on energy or sense bad energy from others.

Begin to reintroduce slight movement into your body, and then open your eyes when you're ready.

This positive energy guided meditation is now complete.

Visualization of a rainbow and a pot of gold

To begin, go somewhere quiet and calm where you won't be interrupted for at least 30 minutes. This is your chance to shine, so take advantage of it. Turn off your phone, put a do-not-disturb sign on the door, and surrender completely to the calm and tranquility that is always present and waiting for you deep inside.

Choose a comfortable position, whether it's laying down or sitting in a straight-backed chair, depending on how you feel today. Take a few deep breaths and concentrate your attention completely to the current moment. Let go of any distracting ideas that are keeping you from connecting with your true self.

Now I'll begin the guided meditation, and when each body part is mentioned, I ask you to bring your mind to it and relax it as thoroughly as possible. If you find stress anywhere when you scan your body, simply utilize the power of your mind to melt it away as effortlessly as warm water melts ice.

Relax your scalp fully, beginning at the top of your head. Relax the skin on your temples and forehead. Allow your eye muscles to relax, soften your jaw, and relax your ears, nose, chin, teeth, tongue, and gums. Allow this serene sensation to run down your neck. As it slides down to your shoulders, upper arms, forearms, wrists, and hands, it will soothe your neck and eliminate any stress.

Allow this lovely sense of rest to pervade your entire body. Feel your chest relax, allowing your heart to expand and become more loving, giving, and forgiving. Relax your abdomen muscles and allow the relaxation to go deeper, relieving any tension in your internal organs.

Allow it to wrap around you, immersing you in love and serenity as it relaxes all of your back muscles all the way down to your spine's root. Continue to take deep, smooth breaths. Inhale health, happiness, and harmony; exhale stress, poisons, concerns, or sickness, letting everything that does not serve you to depart your body like a black cloud.

Incorporate this calm sensation into your hips and buttocks. Allow it to trickle down your thighs, totally relaxing your legs as it reaches your knees, calves, ankles, and feet. Allow any lingering tension in your body to drain out your toes, leaving you feeling very comfortable, serene, and relaxed throughout your entire body.

Continue to take long, soothing breaths, noticing how your tummy rises and falls with each inhale and exhale. Take note of how the air seems cooler as you inhale and warmer as you exhale. Imagine a golden incandescent ball of light hovering approximately a foot over your head. Breathe that light in through the top of your head, the center line of your body, and all the way down to your tailbone on an inhale. Breathe that light back up the direction it came and out the top of your head on the expiration. We'll repeat this process three times to start balancing and aligning your chakras.

Begin by visualizing a brilliant red blazing ball of light at the base of your spine, or a red crystal, flower, or fruit if you want. This chakra is associated with well-being, security, and a dynamic presence. As it links you to ground energy, you will feel empowered. You exude strength and vitality. Inhale red and see yourself living your healthy ideal, joyful and grateful for radiant health and unlimited energy, weighing your optimum weight and having a strong, balanced immune system. Feel how amazing it is to have all the energy you require to do all of your favorite activities. You are in awe of this amazing figure that moves so easily and gracefully while still looking so nice. You'll feel better than you've ever felt before. As you proceed up to your Sacral chakra, which is placed between your root chakra and your navel, allow this beautiful red chakra to continue to shine and spin.

A brilliant blazing orange ball of light may be seen here. Money, power, sensuality, and creativity are all represented by the energy of this chakra. Inhale a rich, brilliant orange hue and enjoy the blessings of happiness, enthusiasm, sexual fulfillment, prosperity, and plenty. Imagine yourself feeling genuine richness on all levels, being grateful for the abundance in your life right now, and seeing riches pour to you in both expected and unexpected ways. As you proceed up to your Solar chakra, a few inches above your navel, let this chakra continue to light and spin.

Visualize a lemon or a sunflower, or a gorgeous sunny yellow blazing ball of light. Feel your excitement, self-worth, and personal power grow as you breathe in a vivid yellow color. Imagine yourself at your dream career, where you are successful and truly fulfilled. As you proceed up to your Heart chakra in the center of your chest, feel empowered by the brilliant yellow chakra and envision a beautiful emerald green or soft pink shimmering ball of light.

This is the chakra of self-love and love for others. Allow it to shine, providing compassion, self-acceptance, and the ability to love truly as gifts. Take a deep breath of pink or green and visualize yourself living in perfect harmony with everyone in your life. Allow it to fill you with gratitude for the chance to live in such a beautiful place. Feel compassion and forgiveness fill up in your heart for yourself and others. Allow this chakra to continue to shine and spin while you visualize a lovely blue hue moving up to your Throat chakra, which is located at the base of your throat. This chakra allows you to speak truthfully and wisely, as well as confidently express oneself. Imagine yourself cheerfully expressing your uniqueness through a creative outlet you like, such as singing, dancing, playing a sport, or anything else you enjoy doing for enjoyment while breathing blue in and out. Allow this chakra to continue to light and spin as you make your way up to your 3rd eye chakra, which is positioned in the center of your forehead.

A lovely deep purpley blue indigo-colored blazing ball of light appears. It increases your creativity, psychic powers, inner understanding, and wisdom as it shines.

Feel completely supported by the Universe as you work toward your personal development goals, joyfully pursuing your highest path. Imagine yourself living your ideal in the area of personal development, whatever that means to you.

As you gradually go up to your Crown chakra at the top of your head, allow this indigo light to continue to shine and spin. Spirituality, thinking, and service to others are all represented by this chakra. Allow this chakra to shine with violet, white, gold, or silver breaths as it delivers gifts of self-awareness, spiritual connection, and happiness. Imagine yourself living in knowledge and awareness, submitting to divine love, and cheerfully contributing to the world in your own unique manner. As you return your focus to the golden blazing light above your head, let this chakra to shine and spin. Keep an eye on it as it develops into a golden Pot. Breathe it in via your crown chakra, Throat chakra, Heart chakra, Solar and Sacral chakras, and all the way down to your root chakra. Breathe it back up the direction it came on exhalation. As it goes through each chakra, the pot fills with gold coins, symbolizing each one's gifts and traits.

Visualize the lovely Pot of Gold above your head brimming with gleaming gold coins once more. This is your one-of-a-kind pot of gold, brimming with everything you could ever desire. Allow them to pelt you. Spend as much time as you like in this meditative state, envisioning all of your desires coming true as you claim your pot of riches.

Healing, tranquility, and peace

Let's start by becoming aware of the breath while sitting comfortably or lying down with your eyes closed......

Feel the air as it enters with a chilly sensation before gradually warming as it goes down into the lungs....

Deep inhale to send energy, vigor, and prana, the life force, into the lungs.....

Feel the body release toxins, tension, and whatever negativity that has gathered as you exhale.....

For 10 deep inhalations and exhalations, stay with this breath, concentrating on the sense of deep tranquility....

Feel the flow of energy throughout your body....

Become mindful of every cell's warmth and tingling sensations.....

Feel the energy that exists in the larger world, in all of nature, and in all living things.....

Bring all of those energy together and sense them as if they were one....

Consider all of that energy as the sun, beaming brilliantly.....

Bring the dazzling energy's gleaming radiance to the summit of the head.....

Feel it begin to descend into your body from the top of your head, gently moving down into your face and neck, down into your shoulders, all the way down into your arms, all the way down to your fingertips.....

Feel the healing energy and light flowing down your spine and through your chest, all the way to your hips.....

Feel it go all the way down your legs to your toes.....

The heavenly healing light and energy has now entered your entire body.....

Allow any physical place in need of healing energy to be totally filled with that healing energy.....

It will warm, heal, and grow across the region......

Allow the healing light to provide calm and healing to any emotional or trauma-related concerns....

Bring any intents or ambitions to the forefront of your mind.....

Hold those intents or aspirations in your mind while you enable the healing energy to bring your deepest desires and intentions to life.....

Know that you are connected to divine energy and light, and that everything is ONE.

Continue to feel blissful, deep, soothing, and tranquil.

Meditation on Body Awareness

Assume your typical meditation position to begin this body awareness meditation. This might be seated or led down, depending on your preference. Close your eyes and take a few deep breaths in through your nose and out through your mouth once you're situated and comfortable.

Concentrate on the feelings that come with breathing. The way the air feels chilly when you breath and warm when you exhale, the way your stomach expands as it takes in oxygen, and the vitality that oxygen gives your body.

Do not be concerned if your mind wanders away from your attention; simply allow yourself to concentrate on your breathing.

When you're ready, move your concentration away from your breathing and toward your entire body. If you have any aches, pains, or stiffness, stretch these areas of your body until they feel as natural as possible.

Now it's time to concentrate on particular body parts, starting with the feet. You may notice that when you concentrate on various portions of your body, they get warmer and more relaxed. Imagine your feet as your body's roots, drawing awareness up from the ground and into the rest of your body.

Allow this awareness to spread up your legs, from your toes to your ankles. Enjoy the pleasant, relaxing sensation. Feel how much heavier and looser your lower legs appear to be than usual. Allow your awareness to travel to your knee joints at this point. If you're having trouble with your knees (or any other area of your body), use this time meditation to imagine your body repairing itself as you move from point to point. Meditation on Body Awareness

Slowly expand your awareness to include your upper legs, hips, buttocks, and genitals. Many individuals find that they keep a lot of their stress in these locations, so take some additional time to relax and release these sections of your body, enabling the energy and awareness to flow through.

Draw this energy and awareness to the base of your spine when it feels correct. It's critical to take your time or your muscles may stiffen up.

Concentrate this awareness up your spine's curvature to the tip of your spine, which is about an inch below the knuckle-like bump on the back of your skull. Relax and ease the muscles around this area, including loosening your jaw if you haven't done so already.

Keep this upper point of your spine in mind while simultaneously focusing on the base of your spine after you've gotten a feel for it. At the top and bottom of your spine, imagine a warm ball of light. Like a loving anchor, the light at the base of your spine is gently dragged down into the earth underneath you. The light at the top of your spine is gradually ascending to the skies. The muscles that support your spine will begin to relax, and each vertebra in your spine will produce a small amount of more space between them.

Shift your focus to your shoulders after your spine is completely relaxed. Because your spine is so relaxed, you may discover that you need to change the posture of your shoulders to be comfortable. Experiment with gently adjusting them into different positions until they feel in line with your overall posture. Draw this awareness down the length of your arms and into the tips of your fingers. Take note of the very minor movements they're making on their own.

Before proceeding up to your face, return your focus to your throat and release whatever tension you may be holding there. Relax every face muscle as you feel the warmth of your awareness. Take note of your face's sensitivity and how the air feels against it.

Finally, turn your attention to your brain. Recognize how incredible and strong your brain is. Your brain has the ability to control every aspect of your body. Your mind, which allows you to think, feel, and create, is housed in your brain.

Open your eyes and return to waking consciousness when you are ready.

Gently Stream script

Lie down in a comfortable posture. If you're seated, keep your feet level on the floor and your hands on your lap, facing the cosmos. Allow the "white light" to begin at your toes and go up your calves, thighs, and hips, whirling and healing as it goes. Allow it to rise to your belly and chest, then drop down to your shoulders. This "white light" will go all the way to your fingertips before returning to your shoulders. You feel it go up to your throat, then up to your third eye, which opens up. Then it'll move to your crown and start raining all over you. Take a look at how lovely this light is!

You can see a way ahead of you. What a lovely route! It's a lovely day. A mild wind and the warmth of the sun may be felt. The trail takes you through the woods. As you go in, you'll notice the chill and hear the birds greeting you. As you go along, you can smell the dirt beneath your feet and hear any little twigs snapping. The light shines through the lovely glistening foliage. The sound of water may be heard in the distance. As you approach it, you realize you've been here before. It's a river with a canoe waiting for you at the water's edge. You can feel the water holding it as you step into it. You settle in and begin paddling. You can see the rings coming out of the paddle when you dip it into the water. Listen to the water lapping up against the boat and the paddle dripping. Take a glance at the coastline and observe how calm it is; are there any animals along the water's edge or birds soaring above you? Take a breath and relax. Make use of all of your senses.

If you're exhausted, lie down in the river's depths and enjoy the tranquility. Listen to the sounds and feel the soft movement.

This canoe will lead you to a route where you may continue. As you go, you notice someone reaching out to shake your hand. Take his hand in yours. You're familiar with him or her. Walk beside them and allow your heart to expand. Pay attention to what they're saying. It may be as simple as one word... You'll understand what I'm talking about. Thank you.

This path returns you to your starting point via the forest. Wiggle your fingers and toes when you're ready, then return.

Angel Healing meditation

Please begin by clearing your laps of all items.

Close your eyes and choose a comfortable position.

Inhale deeply through your nose and gently exhale through your mouth.

Take another big breath in through your nose, then exhale gently this time.

Take another deep breath and hold it for a moment..... Allow your exhalation to be longer than your inhalation.

Now, go deep inside yourself to that point of serenity, love, and oneness with GOD.

Consider yourself on a route winding through a vast forest. The trees are beautiful and towering. You stroll down a soft road made out of earth, fallen leaves, pine needles, and moss. Your body relaxes as you stroll, and you wonder at the beauty of your surroundings...... so serene...... so lovely... Small flowers bloom all along the walkway, and large ferns abound. The air is calm, and a slight whiff of pine and fresh air fills the room.... As you soak in the beauty of this gorgeous woodland, you can hear distant bird tweeting and gentle leaf rustling. Like large shafts of radiant gold, sunlight penetrates through the tall trees and onto the forest floor. As you continue walking, you notice a little wind. The light wind causes the leaves on the trees to swing and move. You are at ease..... As you go down this route, you notice a beautiful ray of sunshine ahead of you.... as you get closer, you notice it's a vast white stairway leading up through the clouds towards the skies. The stairwell is so brightly lit that it glistens in the sunshine. You take a step forward and begin to ascend this gleaming stairway. As you take one step after another, you'll notice how easy it is to climb while also noting how high each step takes you. As you continue climbing, you can see the tops of the trees on either side as you get higher and higher. ..... Soon, the woodland below takes on the appearance of a little green emerald..... You take another step forward as you get higher.... And you'll be able to see through the clouds... As you step through, you are greeted by a chilly mist and the sight of a gigantic domed Temple of sparkling white pearl with eight great columns supporting a bright gold dome. The temple is perched atop the clouds.

As you enter this vast temple, you will notice big cushions placed over the floor in a long row in front of you.... These cushions are the darkest purple tone and glisten with elegance. As you walk over to a pillow and take a seat, you take in the beauty of the temple.

Each massive column is encircled with a deep green vine and the most vibrantly colorful blooms. The sky is a gentle pink with subtle lavender colors that can be seen through each column. This temple's hallowed tranquility is palpable. As you look around, a swarm of Angels descends from the skies and enters through each of the columns' openings. Their big wings fluttering beautifully.... Their cheeks glowing with affection.... Their auras are so bright... ..... They take their places behind each person seated on the cushion, one by one... Their love is so overpowering..... their energy is so relaxing..... They kneel behind each of you on the pillow in unison and slowly bend their heads,....... as their hands clasp in prayer, their giant wings gradually unfold and envelop over you... .... You're surrounded by an ocean of unconditional love and pleasure.... Let us take a minute to express our gratitude to our CREATOR. PAUSE....

As we come to the conclusion of our time of healing and prayer, the Angels softly unfold their wings from over us and stand..... as we stand and turn around, they gently touch the side of our faces, and we know...

EVERYTHING IS FINE.

As we walk away from our cushion, we turn back to the entrance and see the folks we've been thinking about for healing. .... One by one, they enter the room and take a seat on a pillow. It's reassuring to see these lovely heavenly creatures standing behind each human... .....

They kneel and drop their heads once again in perfect harmony..... as they clasp their hands in prayer, their strong wings expand out and fold around each individual you've requested for healing. Let us lower our heads and pray with the Angels for a time.

PAUSE.....

As you conclude your prayer, you notice each Angel slowly unfurl their wings and rise up. The Angels take the persons on the pillows' hands and tenderly hold them for a brief period while they stand and turn... The Lord has heard our prayers.... That is correct.

As you begin to make your way to the stairwell, you turn around to behold these lovely individuals.....

The Angels have gathered in a big gathering... they make a happy face.... And they say... in the purest of voices that sound as ONE... REMEMBER.... WE ARE ALL ONE.... Peace be with you, and love one another as we love you.....

You take a careful exit from the temple and begin your descent.... This Blessing has filled you with amazement and thankfulness.... You're at ease since you know you're never alone.

With each step down, you have a better view of the forest below... It glistens like a million green lights... As you descend each step, you can see the tops of the trees....

And now you can see everyone who has been healed.... Below is where you'll find me... Someone takes your hands as you form a circle around the magnificent glistening staircase as the final person steps off...... You praise God with your arms raised high.... Knowing that you are never alone and that everything is OK...

You've returned to the present... When you're ready, open your eyes and meditate on the thought......WE ARE ALL ONE...

God's blessings on you...

Script for a healing guided meditation

* *Take a comfy seat or lie down.*

* *Allow your body to rest and relax.*

* *Allow the muscles to extend and soften.*

• Pay attention to any sensations that emerge in any part of the body.

• Recognize them, inquire about their needs, and pay attention.

• Don't pass judgment; instead, be aware of and attentive to the signs your body gives.

• Concentrate your mind on your breathing.

• Pay attention to the depth and rate of your breathing.

• Slow down, soften, and deepen your breathing.

• Breathe in through your nose and out through your mouth.

• As you inhale, let your abdomen area to lift and fall.

• Take a deep breath in and feel it go down to your tummy.

• Take a deep breath out and feel it travel upwards and out of your body.

• Pay attention to your body's sensations and feelings.

• Allow the body to relax and release tension.

• Take a deep breath of love.

• Take a deep breath and exhale the stress.

• Breathe in peace.

• Take a deep breath and exhale the disharmony.

• Take a deep breath and let it cure you.

- *Take a deep breath and exhale the sickness.*

- *Keep your attention on your breathing.*

- *Slow down and deepen your breathing.*

- *Take a deep breath of love.*

- *Take a deep breath and exhale the stress.*

- *Breathe in peace.*

- *Take a deep breath and exhale the disharmony.*

- *Take a deep breath and let it cure you.*

- *Take a deep breath and exhale the sickness.*

- *Let go of all self-criticism and self-judgment.*

- *Concentrate on inhaling joy and love.*

- *Concentrate on letting the body to repair itself.*

- *Allow your ideas to help you recover.*

- *Allow yourself to sigh and let go of any impediments to your well-being.*

- *Concentrate on taking slower, deeper breaths.*

- *Let go of all self-criticism and self-judgment.*

- *Take a deep breath of love.*

- *Take a deep breath and exhale the stress.*

- *Breathe in peace.*

- *Take a deep breath and exhale the disharmony.*

• *Take a deep breath and let it cure you.*

• *Take a deep breath and exhale the sickness.*

• *Make your body calm and quiet.*

• *Allow the body to communicate what it requires in order to heal.*

• *Allow the body to relax even more with each inhalation.*

• *Allow a sense of relaxation and serenity to pervade your entire body.*

• *Be present in the moment*

• *Allow the body and mind to flow in unison, resulting in a feeling of calm and well-being.*

Meditation in Stillness and Centeredness

Be conscious that this is a precious moment for you as you slowly close your eyes and sit in stillness. As you relax your body and adapt your soul, time will slow down and the past and future will become less relevant. Allow yourself to be comfortable with pausing and slowing down. Because you are rejuvenated in this location.

In the light of this peaceful area, the thoughts of the day begin to fade away. These ideas are loosening their grip on us, and we can see them as we gently let them go and set them down for a minute. And now your stillness is becoming a bit more audible.

As you breathe in and out, naturally pausing where you need to and enjoying the calm in that moment, your breathing becomes your attention point. This location, right now, is unaffected by the past or the future. It's devoid of labels and judgment. There are no expectations in this situation. This is a place where your spirit can breathe and your vitality may be regenerated. This is the location where your inner teacher communicates, and it is from here that you may hear and listen.

It's possible that this is the first time you've slowed and stopped today. In the silence of your breathing, observe what this feels like for the next minute, and notice that you are secure and without desire in this place.

(Take a one-minute break)

You'll find that your energy is lighter when you relax in this time. You sense a heaviness in your spirit that was previously unnoticed. And you're aware of how it feels. Feel that energy wrap itself around you like a cocoon. Do not attempt to decipher or comprehend it. But take note of it. As your consciousness comes into focus, your inner vision grows sharper, and you become more aware of it. Know that it's okay if your thoughts wander; gently bring them back to the present moment. You could begin to notice holes in your wandering thoughts. Pay attention to them. Those places when intellect and taught information are bypassed, and the thread of our connection to our soul brushes past the universe's thread as it softly collides in this quiet.

And we take our time listening to the energy that this gives for the following several minutes.

(Take a 3-minute break)

You've arrived because you're supposed to be here. You're paying attention to what your spirit need. And you feel at ease in this vibe, in this peaceful breathing space surrounding you. Allow yourself to take pleasure in it. This is what you deserve, and this is the point at which you can declare, "Right now, I'm OK." You're in this realm of discovery for the next five minutes, and you're listening.

(Take a 3-minute break)

Just appreciate it before the concerns and business of the day creep back in. After that, don't be in such a rush to get them back.

As you open your eyes slowly.

TRANSFORMING YOUR THOUGHTS AND EMOTIONS FOR A WINNING LIFE

Table of Contents

"When you control your thoughts and emotions, you control everything."

Marshall Sylver

"Rather than being your thoughts and emotions, be the awareness behind them."

Eckhart Tolle

"Consider that not only do negative thoughts and emotions destroy our experience of peace, they also undermine our health."

Dalai Lama

"Just as the ocean has waves or the sun has rays, so the minds's own radiance is its thoughts and emotions."

Sogyal Rinpoche

Introduction

Do you experience troublesome thoughts? Do you have difficulty accepting yourself? Do you have difficulty managing your emotions? Most people experience these things at times. However, when these things become common place, they can rob you of your enjoyment of life. You do not have to allow thoughts, emotions, or behaviors to control your life. You can experience self-acceptance and inner peace.

Cognitive-behavioral therapy (CBT) is a form of psychotherapeutic treatment that allows us to detect problematic thoughts and redirect our attention from them. Our thoughts elicit emotions and behaviors that are of like kind. If you have angry thoughts, you will experience the emotions and behaviors that reflect this thinking.

Conversely, if you are experiencing pleasant thoughts, your emotions and behaviors will reflect that quality of thinking. Because of this relationship, changing any of these factors can result in a positive life change.

It is important to understand that thoughts lack any inherent power. It is us who give thoughts their power by giving them our attention. Without our attention, our thoughts become impotent.

Dialectical behavioral therapy (DBT)is a form of CBT. While DBT also considers the relationship between thoughts, feelings, and behaviors, it focuses on the emotional component. For this reason, DBT is most often used by those who want to improve their ability to manage their emotions. One can make better choices by being less reactive emotionally, especially within relationships.

DBT allows us to develop self-acceptance, manage our emotions, and feel safe. By doing so, we can respond more appropriately to situations, especially in relationships. DBT accomplishes this by teaching us how to become mindful of our feelings and validating them. In doing so, one can become more effective in managing their emotions.

CBT and DBT utilize various skills to bring about changes, and one of the skills is mindfulness and relaxation. This program provides a wide range of meditations based on CBT and DBT. You will be guided to a relaxed state where you can become more mindful of your thoughts and emotions. In doing so, you will learn how to reprogram your mind for greater happiness and inner peace.

What is Mindfulness?

To be mindful is to be aware. We become mindful when we focus on the present moment instead of the past or the future. For this program, mindfulness is being aware of your thoughts and feelings and anything else that is happening at the moment.

Breath meditation is a simple meditation for becoming mindful and strengthening your concentration. You can use breath meditation to prepare yourself before doing the guided meditations in this program. You will now do the breath meditation:

Breath Meditation

1. Find a quiet place to sit that is comfortable. You may sit either on the floor or on a chair.
    Pause briefly

2. Close your eyes and allow yourself to relax by focusing your attention on your breath's flow.

    Pause briefly

3. Breathe naturally. As you do, keep your awareness of the sensations that you experience from the movement of your breath.

    An alternative to following your breath is to focus on the rising and falling of your abdomen.

    Pause briefly

4. As you breathe, you will experience thoughts, perceptions, and sensations. These will have different qualities to them. Some will be pleasant, while others may be uncomfortable or even frightening. Regardless of what you experience, do not interfere with them. Do not try to control, change, or analyze it. Become like a scientist who is committed only to observing them.

Pause briefly

5. Anytime that you catch your mind wandering, simply return your attention to the sensations of your breath. Do this as often as necessary without any judgment.

Pause briefly

6. By practicing this meditation, you will become more aware of the arising and fading of thoughts. By focusing on your breath, you deprive your thoughts of the attention you have been giving them. In doing so, you will slow down your mental

activity. When this happens, you will experience mindfulness.

Pause briefly

7. This is the end of this exercise.

Now that we have covered the basics, we will move on to the program. This program as three parts:

Part1: CBT Guided Meditations

Part 2: DBT Meditations

Part 3: Affirmations.

We will begin with CBT Guided Meditations.

Part 1: CBT Guided Meditations

The following exercises are for identifying and challenging those disempowering beliefs that are holding you back from living your desired life. The first meditation involves finding the root meaning of your disempowering beliefs. By understanding the root meaning, you will have greater clarity about what is really holding you back.

Discovering the Root Meaning Behind Your Beliefs

To show you how this exercise works, I will provide you with an example. After each step, follow up with your own question or response.

1. Think of an ongoing challenge that you are experiencing in your life. For my example, I will use: My wife and I are arguing a lot. Now, come up with your own challenge.

   Pause 5

2. My next step is to start a line of inquiry using the phrase "What would be so bad if…." So my first question would be, "What would be so bad if my wife and I argued a lot?" Now, provide your own question.

    Pause 5

3. My answer to that question would be, "Our relationship will become more strained." Now, provide your own response.

    Pause 5

4. I would then use my response and rephrase the question: "What would be so bad if our relationship became more strained?" Now, provide your own question.

    Pause 5

5. My response to that would be, "She will leave me." Now, provide your own response.

    Pause 5

6. I would continue to repeat this question by asking: "What would be so bad if she left me?" Now, provide your own question.

Pause 5

7. My answer to that would be, "I would be alone." Now, provide your own response.

Pause 5

8. What would be so bad if I were alone? Now, provide your own question.

Pause 5

9. My answer to the question would be, "I would feel that I am not lovable." Now, provide your own response.

Pause 5

Keep going through this line of questioning until you cannot go any further. When you have reached this point, you will have identified the root meaning of your belief.

In my example, I believe that my wife and I are arguing a lot. This belief is what registers at my conscious level. However, the root meaning behind that belief is that I feel unlovable.

The root meaning is usually found at the level of the subconscious. If you understand the root meaning behind your belief, you are more likely to find a way to deal with your challenge successfully.

Going back to my example, I am more likely to be successful in healing my marriage if I am aware of the fact that I feel unlovable than if I believe that the challenge is that we are arguing a lot.

When you have identified the belief that is holding you back, you can replace it with an empowering belief, which is the purpose of the next exercise.

Challenging Your Beliefs

The main purpose of CBT is to challenge one's limiting beliefs. When we replace our limiting beliefs with empowering ones, we will also change how we feel about ourselves. This exercise will guide you in identifying your limiting beliefs and how to replace them with empowering ones.

Unlike the other exercises in this program, this exercise will require doing some writing. If needed, stop this program and get a piece of paper and a writing instrument. Also, this exercise will require you to get in touch with your emotional pain. This is necessary to replace it with an empowering belief.

1. To begin, write down your beliefs about your life that is causing you unhappiness. When you have created a list, choose the belief that you believe most impacts you. **Pause 2 minutes**

2. When you have selected a belief, sit down comfortably and close your eyes.

Pause 5 seconds

3. Pay attention to your breath as you breathe. Feel it as it courses through your body.

Pause 1 minute

4. Feel yourself becoming more and more relaxed.

Pause 5 seconds

5. I want you to think of the belief that you selected. Feel the heaviness of having lived with this belief all these years.

Pause 5 seconds

6. What has been the cost to you for holding this belief? Consider all areas of your life.

Pause 5 seconds

7. What have been the costs to your emotional health? When you think about that, how does that make you feel?

Pause 5 seconds

8. How has this belief affected your self-esteem? Take the time to feel the pain this belief has created for your life.

Pause 5 seconds

9. What has this belief cost you in your physical health? What has it done to your sense of vitality? Did this belief lead you to engage in risky behavior with your health? How does that feel when you think about that?

Pause 5 seconds

10. Did this belief cost you in your relationships? If so, what happened? Who is no longer in your life because of this belief? How does that feel when you think about that?

Pause 5 seconds

11. What has this belief cost you financially? How does that feel when you think about that?

Pause 5 seconds

12. How will this belief affect your future if you do not change it? If you continue to hold on to this belief, what will your life be like a year from now?

Pause 1 minute

13. What will your life be like five years from now?

Pause 1 minute

14. Now go 15 years into the future. What will your life be like if you continue to live by this belief?

Pause 1 minute

15. Understand that our thoughts and beliefs do not have any power other than the power we give them. Unto themselves, our thoughts and beliefs lack any power. It is we who grant them power over our lives. Further, our beliefs are neither true nor untrue. The question is whether your beliefs support you in living a happy and fulfilling life.

Pause 5 seconds

16. Now open your eyes and get your writing instrument. This negative belief you just meditated on remains with you because you receive a benefit from having it.

Pause 3 seconds

17. Write down the benefits you received from this belief. If you believe that you are not good enough, the benefit may be that it gives you an excuse not to give your all and risk possible failure.

Pause 15 seconds

18. Now think of a belief that will offer the same benefit but will not create limitations for you. Using the previous example, a new belief could be "Success cannot be achieved without failure." Write down your new belief.

Pause 30 seconds

19. When you have written down the belief, sit down comfortably and close your eyes.

Pause 5 seconds

20. Allow yourself to follow your breath. Feel it as it courses through your body.

Pause 1 minute

21. Become more and more relaxed.

Pause 5 seconds

22. I want you to think of the new belief that you wrote down. Think about what your life would be like if you operated from this new belief from this moment on.

Pause 5 seconds

23. How would living from this new belief make you feel about yourself?

Pause 1 minute

24. How would it impact those that you care about? What would your life be like? How does that feel?

Pause 1 minute

25. Think about what your life would be like one year from now if you started to live by this new belief today? How does that feel?

Pause 1 minute

26. What do you think it would be like five years from now? How does that feel?

Pause 1 minute

27. Now go 15 years into the future. What would your life be like if you continued to live by this belief? How does that feel?

Pause 1 minute

28. As you think about what your life would be like, allow yourself to experience the feelings that you experience. Allow yourself to sink into these feelings. You may want to visualize yourself acting from this new belief.

Pause 30 seconds

29. Practice this meditation daily for three weeks. The mind cannot tell the difference between a visualization and actual doing. Making this a daily meditative practice will reprogram your subconscious with your new belief.

Pause 5 seconds

30. This is the end of this meditation. You may remain silent and still for as long as you wish.

It was stated earlier that thoughts have no power over us. Rather, we give power to our thoughts by the attention that we give them. In this next guided meditation, you will explore the nature of thought.

Getting to Know Your Thoughts

1. Sit down in a comfortable position and close your eyes.

    Pause 3 seconds

2. Place your attention on your breath. Feel it as it courses through your body.

    Pause 1 minute

3. Take on an attitude of complete allowing. Offer complete acceptance for whatever arises during this meditation.

Observe the perceptions, thoughts, sensations, and feelings that arise within you. Allow them to come and go on their own accord. All you need to do is to be the observer of them.

Pause 5 seconds

4. Now place your attention on your thoughts. Observe your thoughts as they appear and fade in the space of your awareness. Remain as the observer. Do not judge, evaluate, or analyze your thoughts; allow them to be just as they are. The only thing you need to do is be aware of them.

Pause 5 seconds

5. You may find yourself experiencing racing thoughts. Just acknowledge that your thoughts are racing.

Pause 5 seconds

6. Do not judge your experience; your thoughts have no power other than what you give them. Let your thoughts move about

your consciousness freely. Stay as the observer; nothing else is needed.

Pause 5 seconds

7. Now follow a thought from when it arises to when it fades away. Through your observing, can you find the place from where thoughts arise from? This question is not to be thought about; its answer needs to be observed and experienced by you.

Pause 15 seconds

8. Where do thoughts go when they disappear from awareness? Can you observe this?

Pause 15 seconds

9. Can you know a thought before it appears in your awareness?

Pause 15 seconds

10. If you can observe your thoughts, can you be your thoughts?

Pause 15 seconds

11. You cannot know where thoughts come from or where they go.

Pause 3 seconds

12. You cannot know which will be the next thought before it appears.

Pause 3 seconds

13. Your thoughts come and go, but do you come and go?

Pause 3 seconds

14. You are not your thoughts. Rather, you are the one that experiences thoughts.

Pause 3 seconds

15. Your thoughts have no power over you unless you give them that power. The more that this becomes your experience, the less the impact your thoughts will have on you.

Pause 3 seconds

16. You will now hear a count from 1 to 5. With each count, you will become more awake.

1: Notice yourself breathing in.

2: Notice yourself breathing out.

3: Feel the energy flow in your body.

4: Feel yourself becoming more alert.

5: You are fully awake.

17. This is the end of this meditation. Feel free to remain silent and still for as long as your desire.

Another important part of CBT and DBT is not judging your thoughts or feelings. In the next guided meditation, you will learn how withholding judgments of a situation can lead to new insights and inner peace. This meditation involves relationships; however, you can use the same techniques in any situation.

Meditation for Healing your Relationships Through Nonjudgment

1. Sit down in a comfortable position and close your eyes.
   Pause 3 seconds
2. Now breathe deeply, hold your breath briefly, then exhale.
   Pause 3 seconds
3. Feel the relaxation in your body.

Pause 3 seconds

4. Feel yourself becoming more and more relaxed.

Pause 3 seconds

5. Follow your breath during inhalation and exhalation. Place your attention on your breath. Feel it as it courses through your body.

Pause 3 seconds

6. In a moment, you will be asked to recall a memory that may be unpleasant for you. Know that you are safe and protected. When you recall the memory, imagine that it is a movie and that you are watching it from the audience.

Pause 3 seconds

7. I want you to think of someone you believe treated you unfairly or unjustly. It can be recent or from the past. When you have this person in mind, I want you to relive the specific situation where this person mistreated you.

Pause 3 seconds

8. Where did this situation take place?

Pause 5 seconds

9. Where was this person when the situation happened?

Pause 5 seconds

10. What were they doing at the time?

Pause 5 seconds

11. See all of this in your mind; make it as detailed as possible.

Pause 10 seconds

12. Where were you at the time?

Pause 3 seconds

13. What were you doing when the situation happened?

Pause 3 seconds

14. What did they say or do to you that caused you to be angry or hurt?

Pause 3 seconds

15. How did that make you feel?

Pause 3 seconds

16. Now breathe deeply, hold your breath
    briefly, and exhale.

    Pause 3 seconds

17. Feel the relaxation in your body.

    Pause 3 seconds

18. Feel yourself becoming more and more
    relaxed.

    Pause 3 seconds

19. Follow the flow of your breath as it courses
    through your body.

    Pause 3 seconds

20. Feel yourself becoming more and more
    relaxed.

    Pause 3 seconds

21. I want you to replay the situation in your
    mind a second time. This time I want you to
    observe this person without judgment.
    Observe the situation objectively.

    Pause 3 seconds

22. Where did the situation take place?

    Pause 5 seconds

23. Where was this person when the situation happened?

Pause 5 seconds

24. What were they doing at the time?

Pause 5 seconds

25. See it in your mind; make it as detailed as possible.

Pause 10 seconds

26. Where were you at the time? What were you doing when the situation happened?

Pause 3 seconds

27. What did they say or do to you that caused you to be angry or hurt?

Pause 3 seconds

28. Now ask yourself: "Am I 100% positive that this person intended to hurt me?"

Pause 5 seconds

29. Also, ask yourself: "Is there any chance that I misinterpreted the situation?"

Pause 3 seconds

30. Ask yourself: "Is it possible that I am projecting my thoughts and emotions on this person?"

Pause 5 seconds

31. Now ask yourself this question: "Instead of holding on to my original beliefs about the situation, what new belief can I adopt that will support me and the other person to become happier?

Pause 5 seconds

32. Now breathe deeply, hold your breath briefly, then exhale.

Pause 3 seconds

33. Feel the relaxation in your body.

Pause 3 seconds

34. Feel yourself becoming more and more relaxed.

Pause 3 seconds

35. Follow your breath during inhalation and exhalation. Place your attention on your breath.

Pause 3 seconds

36. We can only behave at the level of awareness that we are at. If we were at higher levels of awareness, we would make different choices. By practicing nonjudgment, we develop clearer insights into situations and respond to them more effectively.

Pause 5 seconds

37. Now breathe deeply, hold your breath briefly, then exhale.

Pause 3 seconds

38. Feel the relaxation in your body.

Pause 3 seconds

39. Feel yourself becoming more and more relaxed.

Pause 3 seconds

40. I will guide you in coming out of your meditative state. When you awake, know that you will be guided by life toward achieving your intention each day. Treat each experience as a teacher who is there to point the way.

I will now count to five. With each count, you will come closer to exiting your meditative state:

1: Notice yourself breathing in.

2: Notice yourself breathing out.

3: Feel the energy flow in your body.

4: Feel yourself becoming more alert.

5: You are fully awake.

This is the end of this exercise.

When we hold limiting beliefs, our confidence suffers. In the same way, increasing one's confidence can dispel these beliefs. This next exercise is for building confidence.

Meditation for Confidence

Confidence is the fruit of learning to trust yourself. Trusting yourself is born from trusting your life. This meditation will guide you in discovering the inner workings that lead to confidence.

1. Get in a comfortable position and close your eyes.

Pause 3 seconds

2. Take a deep breath. Hold it.

Pause 3 seconds

3. Slowly let it out.

Pause 3 seconds

4. Take another deep breath and slowly let out.

Pause 5 seconds

5. Breathe normally, and relax.

Pause 3 seconds

6. Take another deep breath. Hold it.

Pause 3 seconds

7. Now slowly let out. Relax.

   In a moment, you will be guided into deeper levels of relaxation by listening to a count down from 10 to 1.

   When you hear a number, take a deep breath. When you exhale, visualize the number in your mind. Get Ready.

   The countdown will start now:

Pause 2 seconds

   10: Take a deep breath, and visualize the number.

Pause 3 seconds

9: Take a deep breath, and visualize the number.

Pause 3 seconds

8: Take a deep breath, and visualize the number.

Pause 3 seconds

You got the idea. Moving forward, you will only hear the number. You do the rest.

Pause 3 seconds

7

Pause 3 seconds

6

Pause 3 seconds

5

Pause 3 seconds

4

Pause 3 seconds

3

Pause 3 seconds

2

Pause 3 seconds

1

8. Let go of any expectations of what you should be experiencing.

9. Whatever enters your awareness, offer it your complete acceptance.

10. Feel yourself becoming more and more relaxed

11. Sink deeper and deeper into the feelings of relaxation.

12. Become an empty vessel for whatever you experience. The words of this meditation will become the seeds for your growing confidence.

13. By imagining what it would be like to have confidence, the seeds of confidence will sprout and grow.

14. Now imagine yourself in your favorite
place. Where is this place?

Is it a place that you once visited?

Is it in your home?

Maybe it's an imaginary place that you
escape to while daydreaming.

Pause 3 seconds

15. Where ever this place is, see yourself being
there.

Make this place as real as you can.

Pause 10 seconds

16. What do you see in your favorite place?

Pause 5 seconds

17. What do you hear?

Pause 5 seconds

18. Do you taste or smell something?

Pause 5 seconds

19. How does it feel to be in your favorite place?

Pause 5 seconds

20. Go as deep into these feelings as you can.

Pause 5 seconds

21. Now think of a specific time when you felt confident.

What were you doing?

It does not have to be anything complex. Perhaps it was as simple as cooking a meal.

Pause 3 seconds

22. See yourself feeling confident as if it was happening at this moment.

Pause 5 seconds

23. Make this memory as vivid as possible.

Pause 10 seconds

24. What do you see as you relive this memory?

Pause 5 seconds

25. What do you hear?

Pause 5 seconds

26. Is there a taste or smell?

Pause 5 seconds

27. How do you feel when you revisit this memory?

Pause 3 seconds

28. Now make this feeling as intense as you can. Make this feeling the focus of your attention.

Pause 3 seconds

29. Take another deep breath and slowly let it out.

Pause 3 seconds

30. Breathe normally, and relax.

Pause 3 seconds

31. Now think of your favorite color.

Pause 3 seconds

32. In your mind, imagine your favorite color in the form of a ball.

Pause 3 seconds

33. Now return to your memory of when you felt confident.
Make it as vivid as you can.

Pause 5 seconds

34. Place your attention on the feeling that you get when you are confident.

Pause 3 seconds

35. At the peak of the feeling, imagine the colored ball.

Pause 3 seconds

36. Take another deep breath and slowly let it
out.

Pause 3 seconds

37. Breathe normally, and relax.

Pause 3 seconds

38. Return again to the memory.

Make it as vivid as possible.

Pause 3 seconds

39. Place your attention on the feeling.

At the peak of the feeling, imagine the colored
ball.

Pause 3 seconds

40. Take another deep breath and slowly let out.

Pause 3 seconds

41. Breathe normally, and allow yourself to relax.

Pause 3 seconds

42. One last time, return to the memory.

Pause 5 seconds

43. Make this memory as vivid as possible.

Pause 3 seconds

44. Experience the feelings that arise.

Pause 3 seconds

45. Make this feeling the focus of your attention.

Pause 3 seconds

46. Now make this feeling as intense as you can.

Pause 3 seconds

47. At the peak of the feeling, imagine the colored ball.

Pause 3 seconds

48. Take a deep breath and slowly let it out.

Pause 3 seconds

49. Breathe normally, and relax.

Pause 5 seconds

50. Now think of a situation where you would like to feel more confident. When you choose the situation, pick one that does not hold a lot of meaning for you.

Pause 5 seconds

51. Now imagine the situation unfolding.

Pause 15 seconds

52. See yourself entering the situation. As you do so, see the colored ball in your mind.

Pause 5 seconds

53. Feel the energy of confidence as it flows through your body.

Pause 5 seconds

54. See yourself confidently handling the situation.

Pause 10 seconds

55. How do you feel about the situation now?

Pause 3 seconds

56. Take another deep breath and slowly let out.

Pause 3 seconds

57. Breathe normally, and relax.

Pause 3 seconds

58. Now think of another situation where you would like to feel more confident.

For this one, pick a more meaningful situation than the first one.

Pause 5 seconds

59. Now imagine the situation unfolding.

Pause 15 seconds

60. See yourself entering the situation. As you do so, see the colored ball in your mind.

Pause 5 seconds

61. Feel the energy that is confidence as it flows through your body.

Pause 5 seconds

62. See yourself confidently handling the situation.

Pause 10 seconds

63. How do you feel about the situation now?

Pause 3 seconds

64. Take another deep breath and slowly let out.

Pause 3 seconds

65. Breathe normally, and allow yourself to relax.

Pause 3 seconds

66. Now think of another situation where you would like to feel more confident.

    For this one, pick a more meaningful situation than the last one. Select a situation that has been one of your biggest challenges.

Pause 5 seconds

67. Now imagine the situation unfolding.

Pause 15 seconds

68. See yourself entering the situation.

As you do so, see the colored ball in your mind.

Pause 5 seconds

69. Feel the energy that is confidence as it flows through your body.

Pause 5 seconds

70. See yourself confidently handling the situation.

Pause 10 seconds

71. How do you feel about the situation now?

Pause 3 seconds

72. Take another deep breath and slowly let out.

Pause 3 seconds

73. Breathe normally, and allow yourself to relax.

Pause 3 seconds

74. The more you repeat this meditation, the stronger your conditioning will be to experience confidence.

Pause 3 seconds

41. I will guide you in coming out of your meditative state by counting to five. With

each count, you will come closer to exiting your meditative state:

1: Notice yourself breathing in.

2: Notice yourself breathing out.

3: Feel the energy flow in your body.

4: Feel yourself becoming more alert.

5: You are fully awake.

42. This is the end of this exercise.

Many of our bad habits, such as smoking, are formed as a way to distract us from troubling thoughts. By creating a shift in our thinking, we can create a shift in our habits. The following mediation is about quitting smoking; however, it can be used for any behavior you want to change.

Meditation for Quitting Smoking

1. Get in a comfortable position and close your eyes.

   Pause 3 seconds

2. Now, take a deep breath and hold it.

   Pause 3 seconds

3. Slowly let it out.

Pause 3 seconds

4. Breathe normally, and relax.

    Pause 5 seconds

5. Take another deep breath. Hold it.

    Pause 5 seconds

6. Slowly let it out.

    Pause 3 seconds

7. Breathe normally, and relax.

    Pause 3 seconds

8. Take another deep breath. Hold it.

    Pause 5 seconds

9. Slowly let it out.

    Pause 3 seconds

10. Breathe normally, and relax.

    Pause 3 seconds

11. Place your attention on your breath. Make your breath the focus of your attention. Feel the sensations you experience as your breath travels in and out of your body.

    Pause 5 seconds

12. It is normal for thoughts to appear. When
    they do, let them be. Simply return your
    attention to your breath.
    Continue to breathe normally.
    Make your breath the focus of your attention.
    Pause 3 seconds

13. Regardless of how often it may happen,
    redirect your attention from distracting
    thoughts, and focus on your breath.

14. Feel yourself becoming more and more
    relaxed.
    Pause 3 seconds

15. Your mind and body naturally seek to avoid
    that which is unpleasant and pursue that
    which is enjoyable.
    When we are tired, we crave rest.
    When we are hungry, we desire food.
    When we are worried, we want a resolution.
    Pause 3 seconds

16. Smoking creates an unnatural need, the desire
    for more nicotine.

The illusion is that you smoke for pleasure. In truth, you are attempting to meet a self-created need. Meeting this need comes with long-term consequences.

Pause 3 seconds

You may believe that smoking is a source of enjoyment for you and helps you relax. However, this belief is not accurate.

When you smoke, you are experiencing momentary relief from an addiction you created.

To successfully quit smoking requires a change in beliefs.

17. Take another deep breath. Hold it.

    Pause 5 seconds

18. Slowly let it out.

    Pause 3 seconds

19. Breathe normally, and relax.

    Pause 3 seconds

20. Place your attention on your breath as it enters your body as you inhale.

    Pause 3 seconds

21. Experience the sensations that you feel as you exhale.

Pause 3 seconds

22. Notice the calm and stillness that you feel as you observe your breath.

Give appreciation to your breath, for it is what gives you life.

Pause 3 seconds

23. Take another deep breath. Hold it.

Pause 5 seconds

24. Slowly let it out.

Pause 3 seconds

25. Breathe normally, and relax.

Pause 3 seconds

26. Those who smoke do so to distract themselves from unpleasant thoughts.

By smoking, they feel better.

Can you identify with this?

Pause 3 seconds

27. Take another deep breath. Hold it.

Pause 5 seconds

28. Slowly let it out.

Pause 3 seconds

29. Breathe normally, and relax.

    Pause 3 seconds

30. That you can observe your thoughts
    demonstrates that you are not your thoughts.
    You are the one that is aware of thought.

    Pause 3 seconds

31. You are also the one who is aware of the
    breath that flows through you.

    Pause 3 seconds

32. Notice how when you observe your breath
    that your thoughts begin to fade.
    Experience the stillness and peace that you
    feel as you focus on your breath
    Take another deep breath. Hold it.

    Pause 5 seconds

33. Slowly let it out.

    Pause 3 seconds

34. Breathe normally, and relax.

    Pause 3 seconds

35. Now think of how your life would improve if
    you gave up smoking.

36. **Pause 5 seconds**

37. What would you gain?

    Pause 15 seconds

38. How would it feel to be free from this ball
    and chain?

    Pause 5 seconds

39. You can find peace and relaxation simply
    by focusing on your breath. You then can
    find more empowering habits to replace
    smoking, such as exercise.

    Pause 3 seconds

40. How would you feel about yourself if you
    no longer depended on smoking to feel
    peace?

    Pause 3 seconds

41. How would your life improve if you did so?

    Pause 5 seconds

42. See yourself at this moment living this new
    way. How does that feel?

    Pause 5 seconds

43. I will guide you in coming out of your
    meditative state by counting to five. With

each count, you will come closer to exiting your meditative state:

1: Notice yourself breathing in.

2: Notice yourself breathing out.

3: Feel the energy flow in your body.

4: Feel yourself becoming more alert.

5: You are fully awake.

This is the end of this exercise.

44. This is the end of this meditation. Take as long as you want to savor your experience before getting up.

So far in this program, you have learned different meditative exercises to deal with troublesome thoughts. However, another approach is used in CBT that is far more general. It involves learning how to simply quiet one's mind.

Meditation to Quiet the Mind

1. Find a comfortable place to sit and close your eyes.

Pause 2 seconds

2. Take a deep breath, hold it, and slowly exhale. Let the air out in a controlled fashion.

Pause 2 seconds

3. Now breathe normally. As you breathe, place your attention on your breath.

Pause 3 seconds

4. Notice the sensations you feel as your breath travels through your body as you breathe in and out.

Pause 3 seconds

5. Feel yourself becoming more and more relaxed. Enjoy the feeling.

Pause 2 seconds

6. Continue to follow your breath as it enters and exits your body.

Pause 2 seconds

7. Feel yourself becoming more and more relaxed.

Pause 5 seconds

8. As you observe your breath, the mental objects known as thoughts will appear.

Pause 5 seconds

9. Notice how they come and go.

    Pause 2 seconds

10. Do not try to control, resist, or change them.
    Let your thoughts be. Let them appear and
    disappear on their own accord.

    Pause 2 seconds

16. Be like a scientist observing a rare bird. The
    scientist does not interfere with or judge the
    bird's behavior. Be like this when you
    experience thoughts.

    Pause 2 seconds

17. When thoughts appear, accept that they
    exist and return your attention to your
    breath.

    Pause 2 seconds

18. Accept everything that you experience
    without any judgment.

    Pause 2 seconds

19. You may experience thoughts of doubt.
    Perhaps you will have thoughts about what
    should or should not be happening.

Regardless of what thoughts you experience, let them be. Return your attention to your breath.

Pause 2 seconds

20. Feel yourself becoming more and more relaxed.

Pause 5 seconds

21. Notice that your mind and body functions are all occurring without any effort by you.

Pause 2 seconds

22. There is nothing that you need to do and nothing that you need to improve upon. Remain silent as you continue to observe your breath.

Pause 2 seconds

23. Feel yourself going deeper and deeper within. Allow yourself to surrender to everything that you experience.

Pause 5 seconds

24. Your thoughts have no power of their own. Their power is derived from you. You give

them power when you give them your
attention.

Pause 5 seconds

25. Continue to breathe and remain aware of the
flow of your breath.

Pause 2 seconds

26. You are now ready to explore your mind.
You can study your thoughts without
getting involved with them.

Pause 2 seconds

27. To study your thoughts is very simple. It is
just like being a bird watcher observing a
bird from a distance.

Pause 2 seconds

28. To observe a thought is to be aware of it.
Observe your thoughts without engaging
them. You can do this by not judging them
or trying to analyze them.

Pause 2 seconds

29. Do your thoughts change in their intensity,
or do they remain unchanged?

Pause 2 seconds

30. Can you locate the place where thoughts appear from?

Pause 5 seconds

31. Can you find the place where they go?

Pause 5 seconds

32. Your thoughts are constantly changing.

Pause 2 seconds

33. It is not possible to identify where your thoughts come from or go.

Pause 2 seconds

34. Unlike your thoughts, you remain unchanged as the observer.

Pause 2 seconds

35. Unlike your thoughts, you remain where you are when they are coming and going.

Pause 2 seconds

36. You are not your thoughts. You are the one that observes your thoughts!

Pause 2 seconds

37. A calm mind does not mean that you do not have thoughts. Instead, it means that you accept the existence of your thoughts.

The acceptance of your inner world is what creates a calm mind. Enjoy this feeling.

Pause 5 seconds

38. I will now count to five. With each count, you will come closer to exiting your meditative state:

> 1... Feel yourself beginning to awake.
>
> 2… Experience your mind becoming more active.
>
> 3…Feel your body becoming more energized.
>
> 4… Move your hands, feet, and neck.
>
> 5… Open your eyes and feel refreshed.

While CBT techniques are used to manage troublesome thoughts, their use can have an even more profound impact. What I am referring to is our sense of identity and self-esteem. The consistent thoughts that we have of ourselves create our sense of identity, and our sense of identity affects our self-esteem. The next meditation addresses this.

Meditation for Reforming Identity and Improving Self-Esteem

1. Sit or lie down and make yourself comfortable.

    Pause 3 seconds

2. Close your eyes and take a deep breath.

    Pause 3 seconds

3. Slowly let it out.

    Pause 3 seconds

4. Again, take a deep breath.

    Pause 3 seconds

5. Slowly let it out.

    Pause 3 seconds

6. Breathe normally, and allow yourself to relax.

    Pause 5 seconds

7. Before starting this meditation, you will hear a countdown that will guide you into deeper levels of relaxation.

    As you hear the numbers, focus on the rising and falling of your abdomen as you breathe.

    Pause briefly

    10

Pause briefly

9

Pause briefly

8

Pause briefly

7

Pause briefly

6

Pause briefly

5

Pause briefly

4

Pause briefly

3

Pause briefly

2

Pause briefly

1

Pause briefly

8. Feel yourself becoming very relaxed

   Pause 3 seconds

9. If you were to put on yellow-tinted glasses, everything that you looked at would appear to be colored yellow.

    Looking into a mirror, you would see yourself as yellow as well.

    Pause 3 seconds

10. Your sense of identity is this lens.

    Pause 3 seconds

11. Your sense of identity will determine how you see yourself and experience life.

    Pause 3 seconds

12. Your sense of identity was largely learned and shaped by your experiences as you grew up.

    Pause 3 seconds

13. Your sense of identity is a belief; it is a belief that you have about yourself.

    Pause 3 seconds

14. You can change your beliefs. It happens all the time.

    If you no longer believe in Santa Claus, you have a change in belief.

15. Your sense of identity is a form of belief. Because of this, you can form a new sense of identity.

    You can create it intentionally rather than letting others define who you are.

    Pause 3 seconds

16. Take another deep breath. Hold it.

    Pause 2 seconds

17. Slowly let it out.

    Pause 3 seconds

18. Breathe normally, and relax.

    Pause 5 seconds

19. Are you critical of yourself?

    Do you criticize yourself for your shortcomings or failures?

    Pause 3 seconds

20. Now think of someone who you love and care about.

    Pause 3 seconds

21. Can you have compassion for them when they are experiencing difficult times?

22. Compassion arises from within you. You extend it to those who you care about.

23. Can you extend compassion to yourself?
Can you be kind to yourself?
Can you be understanding toward yourself?

Pause 3 seconds

24. To be able to do these things is self-compassion.

Pause 3 seconds

25. Imagine being as compassionate to yourself as you are toward a loved one.

Pause 3 seconds

26. You are laying down the foundation for a more authentic sense of identity.

Pause 3 seconds

27. You are taking a major step in determining who you are instead of blindly accepting the sense of identity that was shaped by the opinions of others.

Pause 3 seconds

28. To form a truer sense of identity, lay down the first brick, the brick of self-compassion. Imagine what it would feel like if you could be compassionate toward yourself.

Pause 3 seconds

29. As you imagine it, notice what that feels like.

Pause 3 seconds

30. Are you able to accept yourself, warts and all?

Pause 3 seconds

31. Acceptance is another necessary component in forming a healthy sense of identity.

Pause 3 seconds

32. To accept your shortcomings does not mean you do not strive to improve.

It means you can value yourself as an individual regardless of your flaws.

Pause 3 seconds

33. You accept your flaws as being part of who you are at this moment.

These flaws are signaling to you the areas of your life that you can build upon.

In this manner, your flaws are a benefit, not something that makes you less of a person.

Pause 3 seconds

34. Lay down the second brick of forming a healthy sense of identity, the brick of self-acceptance.

Pause 3 seconds

35. Imagine what it would feel like if you could be accepting of yourself.

    As you imagine it, notice what that feels like.

Pause 5 seconds

36. You cannot gain self-knowledge if you are critical of yourself or hold on to guilt.

    When we are at war with ourselves, we cannot understand ourselves.

Pause 3 seconds

37. As you learn to be compassionate toward yourself,

    As you learn to be accepting of yourself,

    You are gaining knowledge and self-knowledge.

Pause 3 seconds

38. Self-knowledge is the fruit of learning to be your own best friend.

Pause 3 seconds

39. You are open enough and honest enough to look at all aspects of yourself without being judgmental.

Pause 3 seconds

40. Lay down the third brick of forming a healthy sense of identity, the brick of self-knowledge.

Pause 3 seconds

41. Imagine what it would feel like to learn something about you with each passing day. As you imagine this, notice what that feels like.

Pause 5 seconds

42. As you gain self-knowledge, you are also gaining self-awareness.

Pause 3 seconds

43. To be self-aware is to be aware of your thoughts, emotions, and actions.

Besides becoming aware of these things, you are also becoming aware of how they impact your life and those around you.

Pause 3 seconds

44. This self-awareness leads to further growth within you.

    You are growing as a person because you have built a solid foundation for yourself, a foundation composed of self-compassion, self-acceptance, and self-knowledge.

    Pause 3 seconds

45. Self-awareness is not a brick that you need to lay down.

    Pause 3 seconds

46. Awareness had existed within you before you were even born.

    Pause 3 seconds

47. There can be no experience without the awareness of it.

    Pause 3 seconds

48. Since your earliest awareness, it has been largely monopolized by the world around you.

Pause 3 seconds

49. Now you are pointing that awareness inward.

Pause 3 seconds

50. You are becoming more aware of who you are, the true you.

Pause 3 seconds

51. This true self is a sense of identity not founded on how others perceive you.

It is based on what is true for you and your values.

Pause 3 seconds

52. Imagine what it would be like to be true to yourself.

Imagine what it would be like to live your life that way.

Imagine what it would be like to be solidly anchored in your knowledge of who you are as a person.

Pause 5 seconds

53. Your life has unlimited potential. The more self-knowledge you have, the more you will be able to guide that potential.

Pause 3 seconds

54. You will now hear a count from 1 to 5. With each count, you will become more awake.

1... Feel yourself beginning to awake.

2... Experience your mind becoming more active.

3...Feel your body becoming more energized.

4... Move your hands, feet, and neck.

5... Open your eyes and feel refreshed.

Pause 3 seconds

55. Take as long as you want to savor your experience before getting up.

Your sense of identity is not fixed or permanent. You can change your sense of identity by changing your beliefs about yourself. You can develop a more empowering sense of identity by shedding the old ways of how you see yourself and creating a new sense of identity by adopting the beliefs and taking actions consistent with the new you. Practice this meditation daily till you experience this shift. It will guide you and sustain your focus as you create a new version of yourself.

As a society, our socialization has let us believe that if we make a mistake or do not get the outcome we want, we have failed. However, the concept of failure is just that, a concept. There is no failure in the world; rather, failure is a product of our minds. In this meditation, you will be guided toward a more enlightened view of the concept that we know as failure.

Fear of Failure

1. Get in a comfortable position and close your eyes.

   Pause 3 seconds

2. Now, take a deep breath and hold it.

Pause 3 seconds

3. Slowly let it out.

Pause 3 seconds

4. Breathe normally, and relax.

Pause 5 seconds

5. Take another deep breath. Hold it.

Pause 5 seconds

6. Slowly let it out.

Pause 3 seconds

7. Breathe normally, and relax.

Pause 3 seconds

8. Take another deep breath. Hold it.

Pause 5 seconds

9. Slowly let it out.

Pause 3 seconds

10. Breathe normally, and relax.

Pause 3 seconds

11. Place your attention on your breath. Make your breath the focus of your attention. Feel the sensations you experience as your breath travels in and out of your body.

Pause 5 seconds

12. Before starting this meditation, you will be guided into deeper levels of relaxation. You will hear a count down from 10 to 1.

As you hear the numbers, notice, focus on the rising and falling of your abdomen as you breathe

Pause 3 seconds

10

Brief pause

9

Brief pause

8

Brief pause

7

Brief pause

6

Brief pause

5

Brief pause

4

Brief pause

3

Brief pause

2

Brief pause

1

Pause 3 seconds

13. Feel yourself becoming very relaxed

    Pause 3 seconds

14. Put your attention on your breath as it travels through your body.

    Pause 3 seconds

15. Focus on the sensations you experience as you breathe in and breathe out.

    Pause 3 seconds

16. Feel the weight of your body as you go deeper and deeper into relaxation.

    Pause 3 second

17. A toddler learning to walk will repeatedly fall until it is successful.

    Pause 3 second

18. Crows have been known to drop shellfish on the rocks below to crack them open.

They will repeat this behavior until they are successful.

Pause 3 second

19. A hiker may sense they are taking the wrong path and refer to a compass for the correct direction.

Pause 3 second

20. A spacecraft will be off course as it approaches a planet for landing.

A mechanism inside the spacecraft makes continuous adjustments until the space crafts lands on the predetermined site.

Pause 3 second

21. In all these scenarios, the desired outcome required repeated corrections until it was reached.

Pause 3 second

22. You have adopted the concept of failure.

Pause 3 second

23. You have come to believe that others will see you as being less if you are unsuccessful in

your efforts to accomplish your desired outcome.

Pause 3 second

24. Only in the minds of the human species does the concept of failure exists.

Pause 3 second

25. Multiple trails are undertaken throughout the natural world before the final results are achieved.

Pause 3 second

26. Does not a plant change its orientation until it is exposed to the sun's full light?

Pause 3 second

27. From the point of wisdom, it is impossible to fail or make a mistake.

Pause 3 second

28. Each effort that does not achieve the desired outcome is information.

Pause 3 second

29. Each effort that does not achieve the desired outcome is feedback.

Pause 3 second

30. By consistently paying attention to the feedback, you will eventually succeed.

Pause 3 second

31. If you fear experiencing feedback, you will never achieve your dreams.

Pause 3 second

32. Now say to yourself, "With every failure, I come closer to success." When you say it, say it with meaning. Say it now.

Pause 3 second

33. Again, say to yourself, "I come closer to success with every failure." When you say it, say it with conviction. Say it now.

Pause 3 seconds

34. You will now hear a count from 1 to 5. With each count, you will become more awake.

1... Feel yourself beginning to awake.

2… Experience your mind becoming more active.

3…Feel your body becoming more energized.

4… Move your hands, feet, and neck.

5… Open your eyes and feel refreshed.

Pause 3 seconds

35. Take as long as you want to savor your experience before getting up.

Fear of failure is learned; it is not part of who you are. The fear of failure does not hinder the toddler who makes repeated attempts to walk. Practice this meditation until this fear no longer holds you back.

To be resilient is to overcome challenges and adapt to changes. Rather than being a trait that we are born with, we can learn to be resilient by challenging our traditional thinking. The meditation will guide you toward a deeper understanding of what it means to be resilient.

Meditation for Developing Resilience

\

1. Get in a comfortable position and close your eyes.

Pause 3 seconds

2. Take a deep breath and hold it.

Pause 3 seconds

3. Slowly let it out.

Pause 3 seconds

4. Breathe normally, and relax.

Pause 5 seconds

5. Place your attention on your breathing. Observe your breath as it enters and leaves your body.

Pause 3 seconds

6. You can observe your breath by focusing on the sensations you feel as your breath travels through your body.

Pause 3 seconds

7. Imagine a forest in the wintertime.

Pause 3 seconds

8. Snow falls on the trees and collects on their branches.

Though the weight of the snow on the branches increases, the branch does not break. Instead, the branch bends, and the snow slides off it.

9. Think back to a specific challenge that you
    experienced.

    Pause 3 seconds

10. As you felt the weight of the challenge
    become heavier, how did you respond?
    Did you become defiant?
    Did you try to run or avoid the problem?
    Or did you adapt by bending?

11. Take another deep breath. Hold it.

    Pause 3 seconds

12. Slowly let it out.

    Pause 3 seconds

13. Breathe normally, and relax.

    Pause 3 seconds

14. Feel yourself slip into deeper levels of
    relaxation.

    Pause 5 seconds

15. Do you feel any sense of resistance at this
    moment?

    Pause 5 seconds

16. If you cannot detect any resistance, it is because you are relaxed. You are like the bending branch.

Pause 5 seconds

17. Notice also that your mind is clear.
You make better decisions when your mind is clear.

Pause 5 seconds

18. As you remain relaxed, think about a mild challenge you are currently facing.

Pause 3 seconds

19. As you think about the challenge, maintain awareness of your breath or the feeling of relaxation that you are experiencing.

20. Ask yourself, "What is the best way to address this challenge?" When you ask this question, ask it with sincerity.

Pause 3 seconds

21. After asking this question, return your focus to your breathing.
When the conditions are right, you will receive an answer to your question.

Pause 3 seconds

22. Whatever the answer is, be open to it.

    The answer will not come from a fearful mind; hence, there will be no resistance.

    Instead, it will come from a clear mind.

    Learn to be grateful for both the challenge and the answer you receive.

Pause 3 seconds

23. I will now count to five. With each count, you will come closer to exiting your meditative state:

    1... Feel yourself beginning to awake.

    2... Experience your mind becoming more active.

    3...Feel your body becoming more energized.

    4... Move your hands, feet, and neck.

    5... Open your eyes and feel refreshed.

24. This is the end of this meditation.

To be good at anything in life takes practice. Practice this meditation daily and apply what you learned when you experience a challenge. If you fall back to our old ways of reacting, be kind to yourself. It will take time to adopt a new pattern of thinking. Each time you catch yourself reacting the old way, you will be a step closer to becoming like the bending branch.

Part 2: DBT Guided Meditations

As indicated earlier, our thoughts, emotions, and behaviors affect each other. If we make a change to any one of these factors, the remaining two will also change. CBT focuses on managing thought patterns to change behaviors and emotional states. In DBT, emotional states become the center of focus. DBT helps us become more mindful of what we are feeling and learn how to accept them. Doing so can lead to creating a change in how we feel. When this happens, our thoughts and behaviors will also change for the better.

In the next exercise, you will do the body scan. It is a simple but effective exercise to release stress from the body. For many of us, we are so accustomed to the stress in our bodies that we believe it is normal.

This exercise in mindfulness will give you a sense of contrast to how your body normally feels and how it feels when the stress is removed. The body scan can be done while sitting in a chair or lying on the floor.

Mindfulness of the Body: The Body Scan

1. Before doing the body scan, we will first do a simple breathing exercise to calm the mind.

    Pause 2 seconds

2. Now take a deep breath, hold it, and slowly exhale. Let the air out in a controlled fashion.

    Pause 2 seconds

3. Again, take a deep breath, hold it, now slowly exhale.

    Pause 2 seconds

4. Now breathe normally. As you breathe, place your attention on your breath. Notice the sensations you experience as your breath travels in and out of your body.

    Pause 3 seconds

5. Feel yourself becoming more and more relaxed. Enjoy the feeling.

    Pause 10 seconds

6. We will now begin with the body scan.

    Pause 2 seconds

7. Place your attention on the sensations in your feet.

    Pause 2 seconds

8. Now curl your toes as though you were trying to touch the soles of your feet.

9. Hold it and let go.

Pause 2 seconds

10. Feel the stress leave your toes, and the feeling of relaxation take its place.

Pause 3 seconds

11. Feel your feet becoming more and more relaxed.

Pause 3 seconds

12. Next, place your attention on your legs. Notice the sensations that you experience in your legs.

Pause 3 seconds

13. Now tighten your thigh muscles.

14. Hold it and let go.

Pause 2 seconds

15. Feel the stress leave your thighs, and the feeling of relaxation take its place.

Pause 2

16. Feel your legs becoming more and more relaxed.

Pause 2

17. Now place your attention on your hips and buttocks. Notice the sensations that you experience in these areas.

Pause 3 seconds

18. Tighten your buttocks muscles.

Pause 2

19. Hold it and let go.

Pause 2

20. Feel the stress leave your buttocks, and the feeling of relaxation grow.

Pause 2 seconds

21. Now focus on your upper torso, including your stomach, chest, and back. Notice the sensations that you experience in your upper torso.

Pause 2 seconds

22. Tighten your stomach muscles.

Pause 2 seconds

23. Hold it and let go.

Pause 2

24. Feel the stress leave your stomach area, and the feeling of relaxation grow.

.Pause 2 seconds

25. Focus on your shoulders and arms. Notice the sensations that you experience in your shoulders and arms.

Pause 2 seconds

26. Now raise your shoulders as though you were trying to reach your ears.

Pause 2 seconds

27. Hold it and let go.

Pause 2

28. Feel the stress leave your shoulders as they become more relaxed.

Pause 2 seconds

Focus on your hands. Notice the feeling that you experience in your hands.

Pause 2 seconds

29. Now tighten your hands by creating a fist.

Pause 2 seconds

30. Hold it and let go.

Pause 2

31. Feel the stress leave your hands as the sense of relaxation spreads through your hands.

Pause 3 seconds

32. Place your attention on your face. Notice the
sensations that you experience in this area.

Pause 2 seconds

33. Now raise your forehead until you feel the
tension.

Pause 2 seconds

34. Hold it and let go.

Pause 2

35. Feel the stress leave your forehead as it
becomes flooded with the sensation of
relaxation.

Pause 2 seconds

36. Now take a deep breath, hold it, and slowly
exhale.

Pause 3 seconds

37. Feel your entire body becoming relaxed.
Immerse yourself in the sense of relaxation that
is your body.

Pause 5 seconds

38. This is the end of this exercise.

.

The body scan is a great way to release stress from your body, but how would you like to feel even more relaxed? Learning to relax is an important part of DBT. You will be guided to your tropical beach escape in the next exercise!

Guided Visualization: Tropical Beach Escape

1. Take a deep breath and slowly let it out.

    Pause 3 seconds

2. Take another deep breath and slowly let it out.

    Pause 3 seconds

3. Now take a third deep breath. Hold it. Now exhale slowly.

    Pause 3 seconds

4. Now breathe normally.

    Pause 3 seconds

5. Imagine that you are on a cruise liner. You are on vacation, which is long overdue. You have worked hard for so long, and now it is your time to escape.

    Pause 5 seconds

6. You are out at sea, standing at the ship's bow. All that you can see is the vastness of the ocean and the open horizon above it.

Pause 5 seconds

7. In your mind, see the endless waves that approach you and hear the gentle hum of the ship's engine.

Pause 3 seconds

8. Sea birds hover above you, and you see an occasional dolphin leap above the waves.

    The sights and sounds are making you feel more and more relaxed.

    The gentle ocean breeze and salt spray leave you feeling refreshed and revived.

Pause 3 seconds

9. Take a deep breath and slowly let it out.

Pause 3 seconds

10. Now breathe normally.

Pause 3 seconds

11. Your ship is approaching its destination, an island that few know about.

Pause 3 seconds

12. You can see the island in the distance. The captain has informed you that this island will be your "escape from everything" and that you can spend a full day there.

What do you say to yourself, knowing that you are leaving the rest of the world behind you?

Pause 3 seconds

13. Take a deep breath and slowly let it out.

Pause 3 seconds

14. Now breathe normally.

Pause 3 seconds

15. Your ship is now anchored less than a mile away from the island. It is the closest that it can get because of the reefs. You board a skiff, and it takes you to the island.

When the skiff reaches the island, you disembark. You find yourself on a pristine and secluded beach.

As you walk along the shore, you realize you are the only one there. There is no one around to distract you from the natural beauty surrounding you.

Pause 3 seconds

16. Feel your toes sink into the soft white sand and the sensations of the surf against your skin.

Pause 3 seconds

17. You keep on walking until you find the perfect spot to lay down your towel and do some sunbathing.

Pause 3 seconds

18. Feel the weight of your outstretched body settle on the softness of your towel and the sand.

Pause 3 seconds

19. Closing your eyes, you hear the soothing sound of the surf as it rushes up the shoreline and the occasional squawking of a seabird.

You feel yourself becoming more and more relaxed with the sound of each wave that reaches the shore.

Pause 3 seconds

20. Take a deep breath and slowly let it out.

    Pause 3 seconds

21. Now breathe normally.

    Pause 3 seconds

22. In your mind, hear the sound of a wave. As you do so, feel your body becoming more relaxed.

    Pause 3 seconds

23. Another wave arrives. Feel the stress leave your body as your thoughts evaporate under the sun.

    Pause 3 seconds

24. Another wave approaches; feel yourself going deeper and deeper into relaxation.

    Pause 3 seconds

25. Notice that your breathing is becoming deeper and more full.

    Pause 3 seconds

26. Feeling fully relaxed, you get up from your towel and make your way toward the shore.

You wade into the surf and feel the warm turquoise waters against your skin.

While bathing in the tropical waters, you look around.

In your mind, see the lush green jungles further up the beach.

See the endless blue horizon as you look out toward the sea.

Notice how free your body feels as the warm, clear waters support you.

Pause 3 seconds

27. Now, take a deep breath and slowly let it out.

Pause 3 seconds

28. Take another deep breath and slowly let it out.

Pause 3 seconds

29. How does it feel to be in a deeply relaxed state?

Pause 3 seconds

30. What do you notice when you are feeling relaxed?

Do you feel a certain sensation in your body? How does that sensation feel?

Pause 3 seconds

31. What do you say to yourself when you are feeling very relaxed? Perhaps you do not tell yourself anything, which is very good!

Pause 3 seconds

32. Now take a third deep breath. Hold it. Now exhale slowly.

Pause 3 seconds

33. Now breathe normally.

Pause 3 seconds

34. Though you may imagine that you are on a tropical island, the relaxation you experienced was created by you.

    Know that you can relax by focusing on anything that you find to be peaceful.

To be good at anything in life takes practice. Getting what you want out of this meditation is no different. The more you practice this meditation, the greater will be the results that you experience. For this reason, it is recommended that you meditate daily. Like a sculptor that chips away at a stone, you will eventually reveal your masterpiece!

Emotions are among the most powerful forces to drive behavior. Regardless of how intelligent we may think we are, we have all experienced times when our emotions got the best of us. Ultimately, all of our behaviors have an emotional connection. The feelings that we experience in any given situation can serve as an important guidance system for how we should respond. This is the subject of the next exercise.

Feelings: Your Internal Guidance System

1. Sit down, close your eyes, and relax.

   Pause 3 seconds

2. Take a deep breath, hold it, and slowly exhale. Let the air out in a controlled fashion.

   Pause 3 seconds

3. Do this one more time: Take a deep breath, hold it, now slowly exhale.

Pause 3 seconds

4. Now breathe normally. As you breathe, place your attention on your breath.

5. **Pause 3 seconds**

6. Notice the sensations you experience as your breath travels in and out of your body.

Pause 3 seconds

7. Feel yourself becoming more and more relaxed. Enjoy the feeling.

Pause 10 seconds

8. Allow yourself to become silent and observe the thoughts, emotions, and sensations that arise within. Allow all of these phenomena to present themselves to your awareness.

Pause 15 seconds

9. Relax.

Pause 3 seconds

10. Now think of a situation that is currently causing you concern.

Pause 15 seconds

As you think about the situation, be aware of your feelings.

Your feelings are like a compass; they are pointing out the direction.

They are telling you to move toward or away from what you are experiencing.

Pause 3 seconds

11. When you experience pleasant feelings, it means that what you are doing aligns with your values and with who you are as a person.

Pause 3 seconds

12. When you experience unpleasant feelings, it means that what you are doing does not align with your values and with who you are.

13. What you are doing is going against your personal integrity.

Pause 3 seconds

14. Now return your attention to the situation that is causing your concern.

Pause 3 seconds

15. Ask yourself, "What can I do, believe, or focus on to make me feel better about this situation?"

    Is there a decision that you need to make?

    Do you need to let go of something?

    Do you need to question your thinking?

    Do you need to take time for yourself?

    Do you need to risk disappointing others?

    Pause 3 seconds

16. Keep inquiring with yourself until you have identified a way to address the situation that leaves you feeling a sense of relief, calm, or peace.

    Pause 5 seconds

17. When you come up with a way to address the situation, notice how you feel.

    If the decision leaves you with a positive feeling, trust that this is the correct decision for you.

    Your feelings are accurate for you at this moment in time.

Pause 3 seconds

18. If your feelings regarding your decision change, later on, honor that.

Pause 3 seconds

19. If your feelings regarding your decision remain unchanged, you can trust your compass and the direction that it is pointing.

Pause 3 seconds

20. If you cannot find a way to make yourself feel better, this is also okay.
Allow yourself to remain with the feeling. Offer your feelings your total acceptance.

Pause 3 seconds

21. Accepting your feelings and being at peace with them is an act of self-love and indicates integrity.

Pause 5 seconds

I will now count to five. With each count, you will come closer to exiting your meditative state:

1... Feel yourself beginning to awake.

2… Experience your mind becoming more active.

3…Feel your body becoming more energized.

4… Move your hands, feet, and neck.

5… Open your eyes and feel refreshed.

22. This is the end of the meditation. Please remain in your stillness for as long as you like.

In the next exercise, you will take what you learned from observing thoughts and apply it to your emotions. Awareness of our emotions, which are are forms of energy, is a major step to self-mastery. Just as with thoughts, emotions are energy forms, and they are dependent upon us for their power; they lack any power of their own. All of their power is borrowed from the attention that you give them.

Observing Emotions

1. Sit down and make yourself comfortable.

Pause 2 seconds

2. Close your eyes and allow yourself to relax.

Pause 2 seconds

3. Place your attention on your breath as it enters and exits your body, focusing on the sensations you experience as you inhale and exhale.

Pause 5 seconds

4. Now identify any emotions that you may be experiencing. If you are experiencing a negative emotion, offer it total acceptance. Do not try to avoid it, deny it, or change it; allow the emotion to express itself fully.

Pause 3 seconds

5. Place your full attention on the emotion but do not engage with it. Experience the sensations that accompany the emotion.

Pause 5 seconds

6. Now imagine yourself diving into the emotion; allow yourself to become fully immersed in it. Remember, your emotions have no power as long as you do not try to resist or change them. As long as your involvement with them is restricted to observing and experiencing them, you will be in charge.

Pause 5 seconds

7. What happens to the potency of emotions when you just observe them and allow them to express themselves? If you observe a positive emotion, you may experience its feeling intensify. If it is a negative emotion, you should experience a reduction in its potency.

Pause 3 seconds

8. I will now count to five. With each count, you will come closer to exiting your meditative state:

> 1... Feel yourself beginning to awake.
>
> 2... Experience your mind becoming more active.
>
> 3...Feel your body becoming more energized.
>
> 4... Move your hands, feet, and neck.
>
> 5... Open your eyes and feel refreshed.

Pause 3 seconds

9. This is the end of this exercise.

Emotions are a natural aspect of who we are as human beings. Emotions are forms of energy that we have come to categorize as being positive or negative. Unfortunately, many of us focus on our negative emotions. Focusing on our negative emotions can lead to both mental and physical problems. In this meditation, you will be guided to a better understanding of emotions and how to become less reactive to them.

Gaining Control of Negative Emotions

1. Get in a comfortable position and close your eyes.
Pause 3 seconds
2. Now, take a deep breath and hold it.
Pause 3 seconds
3. Slowly let it out.
Pause 3 seconds
4. Breathe normally, and relax.
Pause 5 seconds
5. Take another deep breath. Hold it.
Pause 5 seconds
6. Slowly let it out.

Pause 3 seconds

7. Breathe normally, and relax.

Pause 3 seconds

8. Take another deep breath. Hold it.

Pause 5 seconds

9. Slowly let it out.

Pause 3 seconds

10. Breathe normally, and relax.

Pause 3 seconds

11. Place your attention on your breath. Make your breath the focus of your attention. Feel the sensations you experience as your breath travels in and out of your body.

Pause 5 seconds

12. Before starting this meditation, you will be guided into deeper levels of relaxation. You will hear a count down from 10 to 1.

As you hear the numbers, focus on the rising and falling of your abdomen as you breathe.

Pause 3 seconds

10

Brief pause

9

Brief pause

8

Brief pause

7

Brief pause

6

Brief pause

5

Brief pause

4

Brief pause

3

Brief pause

2

Brief pause

1

Pause 3 seconds

13. Feel yourself becoming very relaxed

    Pausc 3 seconds

14. Put your attention on your breath as it travels
    through your body.

Pause 3 seconds

15. Focus on the sensations that you experience
    as you breathe in and out.

    Pause 3 seconds

16. Feel the weight of your body as you go
    deeper and deeper into relaxation.

    Pause 3 second

17. As you relax, you will experience thoughts,
    emotions, and perceptions

    Pause 3 second

18. These are natural phenomena that are part of
    your existence.

    Pause 3 second

19. You are about to explore the nature of
    emotions. Any realizations that you make
    regarding your emotions can be applied to
    your thoughts and perceptions.

    Pause 3 second

20. Now notice what you are feeling right now.
    If you are unable to identify the emotion, that
    is okay. To develop a deeper understanding of

emotions does not require you to have the correct term.

Just ask yourself what the emotion feels like. Does it feel negative, neutral, or positive?

Pause 3 second

21. Treat the emotions you are experiencing as though it was a rare bird, and you are the bird watcher.

Pause 3 second

22. The bird watcher does not intrude upon the bird or alter its behavior.

Pause 3 second

23. Similarly, do not try to change, control, or resist any emotion you experience.

Pause 3 second

24. To observe an emotion is to be aware of its existence.

Pause 3 second

25. You are about to be asked a series of questions about what you are experiencing.

When answering these questions, do not resort to logic or your knowledge. Instead, go by your direct experience.

Pause 3 second

26. What can you observe about the emotion that you are experiencing?

Does it have a color?

Pause 3 second

27. Does it have a size?

Pause 3 second

28. Does it have a shape?

Pause 3 second

29. Where is it located?

Pause 3 second

30. Is the emotion you are experiencing confined to a specific space, or is it without boundaries?

Pause 3 second

31. Is the emotion you are experiencing fixed and permanent, or is it continuously changing in its level of intensity?

Pause 3 second

32. As you observe the emotion, is it causing any problems for you?

Pause 3 second

33. Take another deep breath. Hold it.

Pause 5 seconds

34. Slowly let it out.

Pause 3 second

35. Breathe normally, and relax.

Pause 3 second

36. Now think of a time in the past when you experienced this emotion.

Pause 5 second

37. Recall the situation as vividly as you can?

Pause 5 second

38. Can you determine what triggered its appearance?

Pause 3 second

39. How did experiencing this emotion then differ from what you are experiencing now?

Pause 3 second

40. If you notice that your reactivity has diminished compared to the past, it is because

you have reduced your engagement with your emotions.

Pause 3 second

41. You got curious about it rather than getting caught up on it.

Pause 3 second

42. Now say to yourself, "My emotions have no power over me unless I allow them to." When you say it, say it with meaning. Do it now.

Pause 3 second

43. Now say again, "My emotions have no power over me unless I allow them to." When you say it, say it with conviction. Do it now.

Pause 3 second

44. Emotions possess no power of their own. You give emotions their power by getting caught up in them.

Pause 3 second

45. Accept whatever emotion enters your awareness.

Pause 3 second

46. Observe them with curiosity without losing yourself in them.

Pause 3 second

47. You will now hear a count from 1 to 5.

With each count, you will become more awake.

1... Feel yourself beginning to awake.

2... Experience your mind becoming more active.

3...Feel your body becoming more energized.

4... Move your hands, feet, and neck.

5... Open your eyes and feel refreshed.

Pause 3 seconds

48. Take as long as you want to savor your experience before getting up.

Emotions are a natural aspect of who we are. Further, there are no good or bad emotions. It is us who give meaning to emotions. Learn to accept all of your emotions as you would accept a guest. When you accept your so-called negative emotions, they will lose their power over you. Practice this meditation daily until you can do this.

How we are impacted by trauma varies from person to person. Two people can experience the same traumatic event, yet, one can be left untouched while the other suffers lasting effects. How we respond to a traumatic event has a lot to do with the meaning that we give to our experience. This meditation will guide you in modifying your memory of the event in a way that empowers you.

Overcoming Traumatic Memories

1. Get in a comfortable position, relax, and close your eyes.

    Pause 3 seconds

2. Take a deep breath

    Pause 3 seconds

3. Hold it

    Pause 3 seconds

4. Now exhale slowly

    Pause 3 seconds

5. Feel yourself becoming more relaxed.

Pause 3 seconds

6. One more time, take a deep breath

Pause 3 seconds

7. Hold it.

Pause 3 seconds

8. Now exhale slowly.

Pause 3 seconds

9. Feel yourself becoming more and more relaxed.

Pause 3 seconds

10. Take a deep breath.

Pause 3 seconds

11. Hold it.

Pause 3 seconds

12. Now exhale slowly.

Pause 3 seconds

13. Remain silent and still.

Pause 3 seconds

14. Continue to breathe normally

Pause 10 seconds

15. Place your attention on your breath as it travels in and out of your body.

Pause 3 seconds

16. Notice the sensations that you experience as your breath flows through you.

Pause 3 seconds

17. I will count down from 5. With each number, you will experience yourself going deeper into relaxation.

    5: Feel the sensations of your breath entering your body.

    4: Feel the sensations of your breath leaving your body.

    3: Feel the weight of your body.

    2: Your mind is becoming calmer

    1: Feel yourself slipping into deep relaxation.

Pause 3 seconds

18. Take a deep breath.

Pause 3 seconds

19. Hold it.

Pause 3 seconds

20. Now exhale slowly.

Pause 3 seconds

When we experience trauma, the event can live on in our minds. Like a disturbing movie, it replays over and over, haunting us.

Pause 3 seconds

21. Take a deep breath.

Pause 3 seconds

22. Hold it.

Pause 3 seconds

23. Now exhale slowly.

Pause 3 seconds

24. Remain silent and still.

Pause 3 seconds

25. Continue to breathe normally.

Pause 3 seconds

26. Your memories can be compared to a movie, and you can be the movie's director.

Pause 3 seconds

27. During his meditation, you will be revisiting this movie.

Pause 3 seconds

28. Know that you will be completely protected. You will now create your protective zone.

Pause 3 seconds

29. Think back to a specific time when you felt safe or loved.

Pause 5 seconds

30. As you think of this time, recreate it in your mind as vividly as possible.

Pause 3 seconds

31. Where were you at the time?

Pause 3 seconds

32. What did you see around you?

Pause 3 seconds

33. What did you hear?

Pause 3 seconds

34. Was there a taste or smell that you remembered?

Pause 3 seconds

35. As you recreate this time, how does this make you feel?

Pause 3 seconds

36. Focus on this feeling or any specific detail of that time that stands out for you.

Pause 3 seconds

37. This feeling or specific detail will be your
safety zone. Know that you can go back to it
anytime you feel that it is needed.

Pause 3 seconds

38. Take a deep breath.

Pause 3 seconds

39. Hold it.

Pause 3 seconds

40. Now exhale slowly.

Pause 3 seconds

41. Remain silent and still.

Pause 3 seconds

42. Continue to breathe normally.

Pause 5 seconds

43. Before you take on the role of director, you
will first take on the role of an audience
member.

Pause 3 seconds

44. This movie is your recollection of the
traumatic event.
You don't have to see details of what is
happening.

Everyone visualizes differently.

You may not see any images. That is okay.

What is important is that you know what is happening.

Pause 3 seconds

45. See yourself sitting in the audience as you watch the movie begin.

    As you watch the movie, remind yourself that you have a safe zone to go to.

    Pause 15 seconds

    Now that you have viewed the movie, it is time to switch roles.

46. You are no longer playing the role of an audience member.

    You are now playing the role of the director.

    Pause 3 seconds

47. Replay the movie again; this time, imagine that the movie is playing at high speed. To the best of your ability, imagine that everything in the movie is happening at high speed.

Everyone visualizes differently. Visualize the way you normally do. If you are unable to see anything, that is okay. It is enough to know what is happening.

Pause 10 seconds

48. Replay the movie again. This time, run the movie backward.

Pause 10 seconds

49. How does that feel?

Pause 3 seconds

50. Now replay the movie a third time. This time, imagine the specific situation or person that caused harm to you becoming smaller and smaller. See yourself towering over that situation or person.

Pause 10 seconds

51. How does that feel?

Pause 5 seconds

52. Replay the movie a fourth time. This time, imagine that carnival music is playing in the background.

Pause 3 seconds

53. How does that feel?

Pause 3 seconds

54. Now try to replay the movie again as it originally was.

Pause 3 seconds

55. Could you do it?

Did you notice any difference?

Pause 3 seconds

56. Keep practicing this meditation until your memory of the event has lost its potency.

Pause 3 seconds

57. I will now count from 1 to 5. With each number, you will experience yourself becoming more awake.

1: Notice yourself breathing in.

2: Notice yourself breathing out.

3: Feel the energy flow in your body.

4: Feel yourself becoming more alert.

5: You are fully awake.

Pause 3 seconds

58. This is the end of this meditation.

Nothing in this universe has an inherent meaning to it. It is you that gives meaning to all that you experience. You have the power to reduce the potency of your memories by making changes to your memory. Repeat this meditation daily until these changes become fixed in your consciousness.

Sometimes we face challenges that seem insurmountable; this can lead to depression. However, there is a powerful force for overcoming challenges and warding off depression. Your ability to focus your attention is what is behind this force. This next meditation will guide you to this understanding.

Meditation for Challenges and Depression

1. Get in a comfortable position, relax, and close your eyes.

   Pause 3 seconds

2. Take a deep breath

   Pause 3 seconds

3. Hold it

4. Now exhale slowly

5. Feel yourself becoming more relaxed.

Pause 3 seconds

6. I will count down from 5. With each number, you will experience yourself going deeper into relaxation.

    5: Feel the sensations of your breath entering your body.

    4: Feel the sensations of your breath leaving your body.

    3: Feel the weight of your body.

    2: Your mind is becoming calmer

    1: Feel yourself slipping into deep relaxation.

    Pause 3 seconds

7. Take a deep breath.

    Pause 3 seconds

8. Hold it.

    Pause 3 seconds

9. Now exhale slowly.

    Pause 3 seconds

10. What we focus on becomes our reality.
Depression occurs when we consistently
focus on what we believe is wrong with us.
In the same way, you can use the power of
your focus to empower yourself by
intentionally taking charge of your attention
and directing it in a manner that serves you.

Pause 3 seconds

11. In your mind, visualize a red rose.

Pause 3 seconds

12. Now imagine a green frog.

Pause 3 seconds

13. Next, see the face of someone you know.

Pause 3 seconds

14. At no time during this exercise did you
confuse yourself to be the objects that you
visualized.
You did not mistake yourself to be a red rose,
a green frog, or the face of another.

Pause 3 seconds

15. Your visualizations are a form of thought.
Who you are is not your thoughts.

Pause 3 seconds

16. In the same way, who you are is not the thoughts that you routinely focus on.

    Who you are is the one that is aware of these thoughts.

Pause 3 seconds

17. Now place your attention on your emotions. What are you feeling right now?

Pause 3 seconds

18. If you are having a hard time identifying the emotion, that is okay. You can refer to the emotion you are experiencing as negative, neutral, or positive.

Pause 3 seconds

19. As you pay attention to this emotion, notice its qualities.

    Is this emotion stable and unchanging, or does it change in its intensity?

Pause 3 seconds

20. Is the presence of this emotion always present, or does it come and go?

Pause 3 seconds

21. Your emotions are constantly changing, and they come and go.

While observing your emotions, were you constantly changing?

Were you coming and going?

Pause 3 seconds

22. Who you are is not your emotions.

You are the one that is aware of your emotions.

Pause 3 seconds

23. Whenever you experience yourself getting caught up in an unpleasant thought or emotion, remind yourself that you are not your thoughts or emotions.

Confirm for yourself that you are the one that is aware of these things.

Pause 3 seconds

24. Now think of a time when you were kind or loving to someone.

Pause 3 seconds

25. As you think about it, say to yourself, "I was loving to this person," or something

like that. Whatever you say, be sure to start by saying "I."

Pause 3 seconds

26. Next, think of a time when you did a good job on a project. Say to yourself, "I did a good job," or something like that. Whatever you say, be sure to start by saying "I."

Pause 3 seconds

27. Finally, think of a time when you overcame a challenging time.

Pause 3 seconds

28. Say to yourself, "I triumphed over that challenge," or something like that. Whatever you say, be sure to start by saying "I."

Pause 3 seconds

29. When you experience an unpleasant thought or emotion, remove any reference to yourself as you think about it. For example, instead of saying " I goofed up," say, "It did not work out."

Instead of saying, " I failed," say, " success
was not achieved."

Instead of saying, "I feel sad," say, "sadness
is being experienced."

Instead of saying, "I feel useless," say, " a
feeling of uselessness is being experienced."

Pause 3 seconds

30. Now tell yourself, "I take charge of my life
by taking charge of my focus." When you
say it, say it with meaning.

Pause 3 seconds

31. Say it to yourself again, "I take charge of
my life by taking charge of my focus."
When you say it, say it with conviction.

Pause 3 seconds

32. From this point on, take charge of your
focus. Let your attention guide you in the
direction of the happiness that you deserve.

Pause 3 seconds

33. I will now count from 1 to 5. With each
number, you will experience yourself
becoming more awake.

1: Notice yourself breathing in.

2: Notice yourself breathing out.

3: Feel the energy flow in your body.

4: Feel yourself becoming more alert.

5: You are fully awake.

Pause 3 seconds

34. This is the end of this meditation.

How we focus on ourselves can build us up or tear us down. Unfortunately, many of us have not been kind to ourselves for most of our lives. It is for this reason that practicing this meditation daily is important. Be patient with yourself as it takes time to get over your past conditioning.

The last three meditations focused on negative emotions and provided ways to change those emotions. It is important to understand that there are no positive or negative emotions. Emotions are just forms of energy, and energy is neither negative nor positive.

The mind creates concepts like "positive" and "negative." For this reason, the mind can be a powerful tool in determining how we experience emotions. In the next meditation, you will learn how to transform any negative emotion into a positive or neutral one.

Deep Diving Into Emotions

1. Sit in a comfortable position, relax, and close your eyes.

   Pause 3 seconds

2. Take a deep breath

   Pause 3 seconds

3. Hold it

   Pause 3 seconds

4. Now exhale slowly

   Pause 3 seconds

5. Feel yourself becoming more relaxed.

   Pause 3 seconds

6. One more time, take a deep breath

   Pause 3 seconds

7. Hold it.

Pause 3 seconds

8. Now exhale slowly.

Pause 3 seconds

9. Feel yourself becoming more and more relaxed.

Pause 3 seconds

10. I will count down from 5. With each number, you will experience yourself going deeper into relaxation.

5: Feel the sensations of your breath entering your body.

4: Feel the sensations of your breath leaving your body.

3: Feel the weight of your body.

2: Your mind is becoming calmer

1: Feel yourself slipping into deep relaxation.

Pause 3 seconds

11. Take a deep breath.

Pause 3 seconds

12. Hold it.

Pause 3 seconds

13. Now exhale slowly.

Pause 3 seconds

14. We all experience challenges in life, and
    with those challenges, we experience
    emotions like concern, fear, or worry.

Pause 3 seconds

15. We can change how we see our challenges
    by changing how we feel about them.

    Hidden within you is a power that can
transform how you feel about a situation.

Pause 3 seconds

16. Think about something that is bothering
    you.

Pause 5 seconds

17. Now, identify how you feel about the
    situation.

Pause 3 seconds

18. Next, ask yourself what that emotion feels
    like.

    For example, if you feel worried, ask
    yourself what being worried feels like.

You want to describe what the emotion feels like, not what you think about it. To avoid falling into this trap, phrase your response as "It feels like________."

You cannot get this wrong. Go with the first thing that comes to you and trust it.

Keep this attitude throughout this meditation. Here are some examples:

- "It feels hard and edgy."
- "I feel like I want to cry."
- "It feels heavy."

Do it now. Ask yourself what your emotion feels like.

As you do so, pay attention to what you are feeling.

Pause 5 seconds

19. Now repeat this exercise using your response. For example, if you said feeling worried feels hard and edgy, ask yourself what hard and edgy feels like.

    Do it now. Using your response to the last question, ask yourself what it feels like.

As you do so, pay attention to what you are feeling.

Pause 5 seconds

20. Now repeat this exercise using your last response. Example: If feeling hard and edgy makes you feel like you cannot breathe, what does it feel like not being able to breathe.

Do it now. Using your response to the last question, ask yourself what it feels like.

As you do so, pay attention to what you are feeling.

Pause 5 seconds

21. Now that you know how this meditation works, you will continue the rest of this meditation on your own.

Keep following this line of questioning until you experience either neutral or pleasant feelings.

In doing so, you have successfully transformed the way you feel about your challenge.

You did so by diving into your emotions.

You will have 3 minutes before this meditation ends.

Let music continue to play for 3 minutes

22. I will now count from 1 to 5. With each number, you will experience yourself becoming more awake.

1: Notice yourself breathing in.

2: Notice yourself breathing out.

3: Feel the energy flow in your body.

4: Feel yourself becoming more alert.

5: You are fully awake.

Pause 3 seconds

23. This is the end of this meditation.

Whether at the individual or collective level, the heart of all problems is due to a lack of acceptance. Learning to accept ourselves and others is the key to creating a better world. We create resistance when we do not accept something, and resistance prevents growth. Learning to accept your feelings without judgment is an important part of emotional self-mastery. This mediation will guide you to developing an attitude of acceptance.

Meditation on Acceptance

1. Get in a comfortable position and close your eyes.

   Pause 3 seconds

2. Now, take a deep breath and hold it.

   Pause 3 seconds

3. Slowly let it out.

   Pause 3 seconds

4. Breathe normally, and relax.

   Pause 5 seconds

5. Take another deep breath. Hold it.

   Pause 5 seconds

6. Slowly let it out.

   Pause 3 seconds

7. Breathe normally, and relax.

   Pause 3 seconds

8. Take another deep breath. Hold it.

   Pause 5 seconds

9. Slowly let it out.

   Pause 3 seconds

10. Breathe normally, and relax.

Pause 3 seconds

11. Place your attention on your breath. Make your breath the focus of your attention. Feel the sensations you experience as your breath travels in and out of your body.

Pause 5 seconds

12. Before starting this meditation, you will be guided into deeper levels of relaxation by a count down from 10 to 1.

As you hear the numbers, focus on the rising and falling of your abdomen as you breathe.

Pause 3 seconds

10

Brief pause

9

Brief pause

8

Brief pause

7

Brief pause

6

Brief pause

5

Brief pause

4

Brief pause

3

Brief pause

2

Brief pause

1

Pause 3 seconds

13. Feel yourself becoming very relaxed

    Pause 3 seconds

14. Put your attention on your breath as it travels
    through your body.

    Pause 3 seconds

15. Focus on the sensations you experience as
    you breathe in and out.

    Pause 3 seconds

16. Feel the weight of your body as you go
    deeper and deeper into relaxation.

    Pause 3 seconds

17. Drop any expectations of what you should be experiencing.

Pause 3 seconds

18. Do not judge anything that you experience or yourself.

Pause 3 seconds

19. There is nothing for you to do.

    There is nothing for you to strive for.

    There is nothing for you to accomplish.

Pause 3 seconds

20. When thoughts appear, do not engage with them. Just let them be.

Pause 3 seconds

21. Turn your attention to the movement of your breath.

    Let it be your anchoring point to keep you grounded in your meditation.

Pause 3 seconds

22. Notice how your thoughts move in and out of your awareness.

Pause 3 seconds

23. Notice how your perceptions come and go as well.

Pause 3 seconds

24. Notice how your sensations change in their intensity as they come and go as well.

Pause 3 seconds

25. Thoughts, perceptions, and sensations are coming and going on their own without any involvement by you.

Pause 3 seconds

26. Thoughts, perceptions, and sensations come and go.

Are you coming and going at this moment?

Pause 3 seconds

27. You are not your thoughts, perceptions, or sensations.

You are the one that is aware of them.

Pause 3 seconds

28. You only have two choices. You can accept them or resist them.

Pause 3 seconds

29. As you have no control of your thoughts,
perceptions, or sensations, trying to resist
them would be a futile effort.

Pause 3 seconds

30. How do you feel about yourself?

Do you like who you are?

Perhaps you are critical of yourself?

Pause 3 seconds

31. When you like something, that is a thought.

Pause 3 seconds

32. When you are critical of something, that is a
thought as well.

Pause 3 seconds

33. Learning to accept yourself is to embrace all
aspects of yourself without exception.

Pause 3 seconds

34. Both that you like about yourself and what
you see as flaws are just thoughts.

You are not your thoughts.

Pause 3 seconds

35. Similarly, any judgments that you may have
others are thoughts as well.

You cannot accept others until you can accept yourself.

Pause 3 seconds

36. When you learn to accept yourself, you will greet others with acceptance.

Pause 3 seconds

37. To accept yourself does not mean that you do not strive to improve yourself.

Pause 3 seconds

38. To accept yourself is to honor yourself just the way you are and strive to continue to grow as a human being.

Pause 3 seconds

39. Self-acceptance provides the space for your untapped potential to express itself.

Pause 3 seconds

40. Now say to yourself, "I honor myself and embrace all I am." When you say this, say it with meaning.

Pause 3 seconds

41. Say it again to yourself, "I honor myself and embrace all I am." When you say this, say it with conviction.

Pause 3 seconds

42. You will now hear a count from 1 to 5.

With each count, you will become more awake.

1... Feel yourself beginning to awake.

2... Experience your mind becoming more active.

3...Feel your body becoming more energized.

4... Move your hands, feet, and neck.

5... Open your eyes and feel refreshed.

Pause 3 seconds

43. Take as long as you want to savor your experience before getting up.

Acceptance is a word that is often misunderstood. Acceptance does not mean being passive. To have an attitude of acceptance is to acknowledge one's current reality without trying to deny it or resist it. Instead of denial or resistance, embrace your realities existence.

Practice acceptance by finding a way to create value out of the situation. Practice meditation daily until this becomes your attitude.

Learning to accept your emotions without judgment is an important step toward letting go. To let go of our emotions is to acknowledge their existence without getting involved with them. For example, you can learn to experience the emotion of sadness without feeling sad. This next mediation will guide you to this understanding.

Guided Meditation for Letting Go

1. Lie down or sit as straight as you can while remaining comfortable

    Pause 3 seconds

2. Close your eyes and take a deep breath.

    Pause 3 seconds

3. Slowly lct it out.

    Pause 3 seconds

4. Take another deep breath and slowly let out.

Pause 5 seconds

5. Breathe normally, and allow yourself to relax.

    Pause 3 seconds

6. Feel the calmness in your body and mind.

    Pause 3 seconds

7. Let go of any expectations of what you should be experiencing.

    Pause 3 seconds

8. Accept whatever you are experiencing at this moment.

    Pause 3 seconds

9. Sink deeper and deeper into relaxation.

    Pause 3 seconds

10. In this state of relaxation, all mental activity slows down.

    Pause 3 seconds

11. Having a calm mind will allow you to harness the power of your subconscious mind.

    Pause 3 seconds

12. All that we experience is the manifestation of subconsciousness.

Pause 3 seconds

13. Your intentions inform consciousness of what you want it to create.

Pause 3 seconds

14. For this meditation, your intention will be to let go.

Pause 3 seconds

15. Take a deep breath

Pause 3 seconds

16. Slowly let it out.

Pause 3 seconds

17. Breathe normally, and allow yourself to relax.

Pause 5 seconds

18. Now place your attention on your breath

Pause 3 seconds

19. Place your attention on the sensations you experience as your breath flows in and out of your body.

Pause 3 seconds

20. Feel yourself sinking deeper into relaxation as you observe the movement of your breath.

Pause 10 seconds

21. Thoughts will appear. Allow them to come.

Pause 3 seconds

22. Be aware of how thoughts come and go in the field of your awareness.

Pause 3 seconds

23. Notice that your thoughts are functioning independently of you.

Pause 3 seconds

24. Do not try to resist, deny, or change any thought.

Pause 3 seconds

25. Thoughts are energy forms and naturally occur within consciousness.

Pause 3 seconds

26. They lack any inherent power of their own.

Pause 3 seconds

27. Thoughts derive all their power from the attention that you give them.

Pause 3 seconds

28. You are the witness to the movement of thought.

Pause 3 seconds

29. Try now to let go of the need to focus on your thoughts. Do this by placing your attention on your breath.

Pause 3 seconds

30. Let your thoughts come and go on their own accord.

Pause 3 seconds

31. Now notice the functioning of your senses.

Pause 3 seconds

32. Your senses perceive through seeing, smelling, and hearing. All of your senses are operating.

Pause 3 seconds

33. Even with your eyes closed, seeing is taking place. You may be seeing images, movements, lights, or shades of color.

Pause 3 seconds

34. Notice that your senses are functioning independently of you.

Pause 3 seconds

35. Observe how the objects of perception are continually changing in form or intensity.

Pause 3 seconds

36. As with thoughts, they also move in and out of your awareness.

Pause 3 seconds

37. Let them come and go on their own accord.

Pause 3 seconds

38. You are the witness to the perception that is taking place.

Pause 3 seconds

39. Try now to let go of the need to give attention to the objects of your perception.

    Do this by placing your attention on your breath.

Pause 5 seconds

40. Take a deep breath

Pause 3 seconds

41. Slowly let it out.

Pause 3 seconds

42. Now bring your attention to the sensations of your body.

Pause 3 seconds

43. Observe how the body's sensations come and go within the field of your awareness.

Pause 5 seconds

44. Notice how the sensations of the body are continually changing.

Pause 3 seconds

45. The sensations of the body occur independently of you.

Pause 3 seconds

46. Let them come and go on their own accord.

Pause 3 seconds

47. You are the witness to the sensations that you experience.

Pause 3 seconds

48. Try now to let go of the need to focus on the body's sensations.

Do this by placing your attention on your breath.

Pause 5 seconds

49. Take a deep breath

Pause 3 seconds

50. Slowly let it out.

Pause 3 seconds

51. Breathe normally, and allow yourself to relax.

Pause 3 seconds

52. Now consider the concept of time.

Pause 3 seconds

53. Like a river, time appears to be continually flowing.

Pause 3 seconds

54. Notice that the flow of time occurs independently of you.

Pause 3 seconds

55. Remain as a witness to the flow of time.

Pause 3 seconds

56. Take a deep breath and slowly let it out.

Pause 3 seconds

57. Now think about the people in your life.

Pause 3 seconds

58. They also undergo changes and are coming and going.

Pause 3 seconds

59. The journey of their lives unfolds independently of you.

Pause 3 seconds

60. You are the witness to the way that people change.

Pause 3 seconds

61. You are the witness to all of these things and much more.

Pause 3 seconds

62. At an even deeper level, you are even aware that witnessing occurs.

Pause 3 seconds

63. That which is your true self is the witness to how you perceive yourself.

Pause 3 seconds

64. For the next few moments, try to let go of any concepts you may have of yourself.

Pause 3 seconds

65. Trust life, be open to all it offers you, and then let go.

Pause 3 seconds

66. Each day, hold the intention that you will practice letting go.

Pause 3 seconds

67. I will now count from 1 to 5. As I count, you will return to everyday consciousness.

1... Feel yourself beginning to awake.

2... Experience your mind becoming more active.

3...Feel your body becoming more energized.

4... Move your hands, feet, and neck.

5... Open your eyes and feel fresh.

Pause 3 seconds

68. This is the end of this meditation.

In the next exercise, you will use conditioning to bring forth feelings of happiness and inner peace at will.

Meditation for Happiness and Inner Peace

1. Make yourself comfortable and close your eyes.

Pause 3 seconds

2. Take a deep breath and slowly let it out.

Pause 3 seconds

3. Take another deep breath and slowly let out.

Pause 5 seconds

4. Now breathe normally and relax.

    Pause 3 seconds

5. Take another deep breath and slowly let out.
    Relax.

    Pause 3 seconds

6. Feel yourself becoming more and more
    relaxed

    Pause 3 seconds

7. Let go of any expectations of what you
    should be experiencing.

    Pause 3 seconds

8. Accept whatever you are experiencing at this
    moment.

    Pause 3 seconds

9. Feel yourself sinking deeper and deeper into
    relaxation.

    Pause 3 seconds

10. Imagine that you are lying on a tropical
    beach.

    Pause 3 seconds

11. Feel the warm sun on your skin and the soft white sand beneath you.

Pause 3 seconds

12. Feel the ocean breeze softly blowing as you become more and more relaxed.

Pause 3 seconds

13. Hear the sound of the surf as it rushes up the shoreline.

Pause 3 seconds

14. Feel yourself becoming more and more relaxed.

15. Now make those feelings stronger by making them your focus of attention.

Pause 3 seconds

16. Imagine yourself diving into your feelings. Let yourself become immersed in them.

Pause 3 seconds

17. Take a deep breath and slowly let it out.

Pause 3 seconds

18. Relax as you breathe normally.

Pause 3 seconds

19. How does that feel?

20. Fully experience what you are feeling.

21. Take a deep breath and let it out slowly. Feel yourself becoming more relaxed.

22. Breathe normally as you enjoy the feelings of relaxation.

23. Fully experience what you are feeling.

24. Now make those feelings stronger by making them your focus of attention.

25. When your feelings are at their strongest, say to yourself the name of your favorite color.

26. Fully experience what you are feeling.

27. Take a deep breath and let it out slowly. Feel yourself becoming more relaxed.

28. Breathe normally as you enjoy the feelings of relaxation.

Pause 3 seconds

29. Fully experience what you are feeling.

Pause 3 seconds

30. Now make those feelings stronger by making them your focus of attention.

Pause 3 seconds

31. When your feelings are at their strongest, say to yourself the name of your favorite color.

Pause 3 seconds

32. Again, take a deep breath and let it out slowly.

Pause 3 seconds

33. Feel yourself becoming more relaxed.

Pause 3 seconds

34. Breathe normally as you enjoy the feelings of relaxation.

Pause 3 seconds

35. Fully experience what you are feeling.

Pause 3 seconds

36. Make those feelings stronger by making them your focus of attention.

Pause 3 seconds

37. When your feelings are at their strongest, say to yourself the name of your favorite color.

Notice how you feel.

Pause 3 seconds

38. Now see yourself sitting down and facing the ocean.

Pause 3 seconds

39. Watch the waves come in and then return to the sea. See them move in and out.

Pause 3 seconds

40. Your inner world is like that of the ocean.

Pause 3 seconds

41. Like the waves, your thoughts come in and out of your awareness.

Pause 3 seconds

42. Just as with your thoughts, your emotions come in and out of your awareness.

Pause 3 seconds

43. What about the sensations that you experience? Do they not also move in and out of your awareness?

Pause 3 seconds

44. If you see any images, notice that they too move in and out of your awareness.

Pause 3 seconds

45. You are the one witnessing the movement of thoughts, emotions, sensations, and perceptions.

Pause 3 seconds

46. There is an aspect of you that witnesses all that you experience. Unlike what is witnessed, this aspect of you never comes and goes.

Pause 3 seconds

47. Inner peace comes from knowing that you are the witness to all things.

Pause 3 seconds

48. You are like the sky, while your thoughts, emotions, sensations, and perceptions are like the passing clouds.

Pause 3 seconds

49. The sky fully accepts the clouds and remains undisturbed by them. By doing the same, your inner peace is revealed.

Pause 3 seconds

50. Now take a deep breath and let it out slowly.

Pause 3 seconds

51. Now say to yourself the name of your favorite color.

Pause 3 seconds

52. How does that feel?

Pause 3 seconds

53. Did you experience a change in the way you felt?

Pause 3 seconds

54. The more you repeat his meditation, the more powerful the change you will experience when you say your color's name.

55. Enjoy the feelings of stillness, happiness, and inner peace.

Pause 3 seconds

56. Take as long as you want as you savor your experience. When you are ready, open your eyes.

Part 3: Affirmations

Affirmations are empowering statements that we make to ourselves with a sense of conviction. By repeating affirmations, one creates a new focal point for the attention. The increased attention leads to the affirmation becoming established in one's belief system. Each time you repeat an affirmation, you strengthen your beliefs about what is true. You are also strengthening your vision of what your life can become. The reason for this is that repeating affirmations rewires your brain.

When you first start repeating affirmations, it may seem like you are just going through the motions. You may feel that nothing much is happening, that you are just repeating words.

If this is your experience, do not be disappointed as this is normal. Repeat your affirmations as often as you like. The more you repeat them, the more ingrained they will become in your consciousness.

It takes about a month of a consistent repeating of affirmations before you will notice any changes. One of the changes you will notice is that the affirmation will replace your limiting beliefs. Your mind will become conditioned for empowering thoughts. If a negative thought appears, your affirmation will automatically take its place.

To be effective, affirmations need to be experienced emotionally. Many people make the mistake of simply repeating the affirmation to themselves, which has little power. To be effectively used, affirmations need to be accompanied by emotional intensity. When you repeat an affirmation to yourself, say it as you mean it!

For this reason, you must choose an affirmation that you believe in. You need to believe what you are saying. If you do not believe in the affirmation, you will just be repeating words.

When reciting affirmations, you may feel a sense of calm or relief. If that is the case, you have selected a good affirmation for yourself. The following are suggestions for using affirmations:

- Choose affirmations that resonate with you. You want to select affirmations that are meaningful to you. You also want to choose an affirmation that matches the outcome you want to achieve.

- Affirmations work better when you can hear yourself speak the words. Say your affirmation out loud while standing before a mirror. Do this for five minutes, three times a day.

- You can also write out your affirmations in your journal. Writing them out or saying them aloud is superior to just thinking about them. When writing your affirmations, focus on one affirmation at a time. As with reciting your affirmation, the more you write it out, the better.

- Visualize your affirmations as though you were experiencing them in your current reality.

  When visualizing, see yourself thinking and behaving consistently with your affirmation.

The following are affirmations for CBT & DBT:

.

My dignity and worth as a human being are granted by my creator.

I deserve to be here

I deserve the chance to make a difference in my world.

I am worthy of respect.

I am worthy of an opportunity.

I am intelligent and wise.

I am liberating myself from the chains of my negativity.

I am intelligent and capable.

I am worthy because I exist.

I deserve all the good things that come to me.

I take responsibility for my health.

I take time for self-care because I am worth it.

I honor myself by being true to who I am.

I have something to give to this world.

I have something to contribute to the making of a better world.

I celebrate life for giving me life.

I stand up for life, for life is sacred.

I embrace the abundance that life has to offer.

I am a good person, and I am worthy.

I am a source of love, strength, and faith.

I honor and believe in myself.

I have something to offer the world.

I am grateful to be born into life.

I am growing as a person

I deserve a place at the table.

I deserve to be part of the conversation.

I am more than enough to be successful.

I am good enough just being me.

I will honor my pain.

I validate my feelings because they are my connection to my soul.

I am worthy of all good things in life.

My life matters, for it comes from the source of life itself.

I am worthy of respect and dignity.

I am worthy of appreciation.

I love myself for who I am.

I am worthy of success.

I am determined to be successful.

I am committed to achieving my dreams.

I forgive myself.

I am committed to my success.

I am blessed with love.

I celebrate my life and the life of others.

I am worthy of being cherished.

How I feel is a decision that I make.

I forgive the past and embrace the future.

I am in control of my mind.

I love myself.

I love the way I look.

I take care of my health, for it is a gift from my creator.

I am powerful.

I love living healthfully.

I take care of myself emotionally and physically.

I am where I am supposed to be at this moment. It is my starting point for greatness.

I add value to this world.

I love challenging myself.

I give and embrace love.

I am breaking through the bondage of lies that I was told.

I am passionate about living healthfully.

I am blessed to be alive.

I am becoming stronger and wiser.

I am in charge of my health.

I am focused and disciplined.

My love and wisdom run deep.

I am blessed with good fortune.

I am blessed with love.

I am becoming healthier and stronger.

I am the captain of my destiny.

I respect myself, and I respect life.

I love myself and my life.

My life is radiant; like a precious jewel, it shines.

I am blessed with hidden talents.

In the art of life, I am a masterpiece.

I have everything that I need

I am prosperous in heart and spirit.

I am proud of who I am.

I have boundaries because I respect myself and others.

I am open to life.

What I think matters.

What I have to say matters.

I determine how I define myself.

I seek help because we are all connected and support each other.

I love myself just the way I am.

I am grateful for all of my life's experiences.

I believe in myself because I am an expression of my creator.

I am valuable because I have something to give.

I am in tune with myself.

I practice self-care.

I am a great person because of who I am.

I am adventurous and fun-loving.

I love being me.

I am worthy; I deserve all good things that come to me.

I am loved, and I love.

I am compassionate and caring.

I do not have to explain or justify who I am. I am worthy of respect just the way I am.

I choose to be happy and successful.

I have no need to impress others or to prove myself.

I am worthy of happiness for just being me.

I accept and love myself for who I am.

I take time for myself because I deserve it.

I am worthy of happiness.

Today, I will believe in myself.

I am worthy of all my desires.

I set boundaries for myself out of respect for myself.

I spend time centering myself.

I set boundaries out of respect for myself and others.

I am a loving and supportive friend.

I am healthy, strong, and beautiful.

I strive for only the best for myself and others.

I am a loving soul, and I am loved by others.

My strength is in my vulnerability.

I can love others because I love myself.

I do not have to do anything to prove my self-worth.

I belong where ever I am.

I always win when I am being myself.

I am loved and supported by the universe.

My self-worth is without conditions.

I am gentle and caring with myself throughout life's changes.

I honor my feelings, for they are valid.

I heal myself by allowing myself to experience all that I feel.

I trust in my ability to succeed, and I believe in myself.

Within me lies the power and great strength, and I am learning to express it.

I do not let others' opinions of me shake my sense of dignity and self-worth.

I accept that others may have opinions that clash with mine.

I do not engage in spreading gossip or untruths about others.

I am no less and no more deserving of good things than others.

I am good enough and worthy enough.

I am. Enough said.

I accept that prejudice and sexism exist, but I will not hold on to hate or resentment.

I provide support to others in a way that is consistent with my self-respect and dignity.

I embrace my gifts, talents, and strengths.

I can offer new perspectives and ideas that reflect my experience.

I will use the perceptions that others have of me to empower me. I will never let the perceptions of others make me feel less.

I let go of the need to impress others, for I have nothing to prove. I am perfect just as I am.

I honor my need for rest and relaxation. I will honor myself by taking time daily for "me time."

I love the way that I look. I love all of my features, including my imperfections.

I offer value to people. I am a valuable resource for them.

I enjoy showing others who I am and what I can offer.

I take time for myself to relax and have a break. I treat self-care as a priority.

I love myself, and I treat myself with respect. For this reason, I do not take on more than I can handle.

I am comfortable saying "no" when it is necessary.

My time is valuable, and I deserve to spend it as I choose.

I bring a unique perspective to the table, as well as my unique background.

I am greeted by my creator's love every morning, and I am renewed.

The strength and love of my creator reside within me at every moment.

I am confident and strong.

I am filled with the love and energy of the universe, and it renews me.

I am proud of who I am.

I am a gentle soul.

I am a force for good.

My feelings count.

My life matters.

I honor my feelings.

I honor my beliefs.

I am intelligent and wise.

I am worthy of being where I am.

I deserve everything that I have attained.

I deserve to take care of myself because I work hard.

I am good enough just as I am, yet, I strive to improve each day.

I embrace my sexuality.

I am forgiving and accepting of myself, and I move forward with my life.

I am like a masterpiece. I am a classical work of art.

I have no need to impress others as I have nothing to prove. I fully accept myself.

I do not compare myself to others; I only judge myself by how far I have come in becoming a better version of myself.

I am a strong and resilient woman.

I choose to feel happy. I have the power to do so, and I have the right.

I do not allow anyone in my life to disturb my sense of emotional wellbeing. I will replace them with those with who I share a connection.

I affirm my humanity and allow myself to experience all of my emotions, make mistakes, fail, and succeed.

I let go of my guilt, resentments and hurts and opened myself to healing.

Final Words

You have been presented with a wealth of information in this program for changing your thoughts and feelings. This program is not intended to be a one-time listen. Rather, it is intended to be a long-term companion you can turn into when needed. The following are some suggestions for getting the most out of your experience:

- Do not judge anything that you experience.
- Do not hold expectations of what should happen or what should not happen.
- Allow everything that you experience to happen; do not resist anything. Every thought and emotion has its place.
- No thought or sensation can harm you. It is you to whom they owe their existence.

Having said this, here are some suggestions regarding the content in this program:

- Ensure that you listen to the entire program and do each meditation at least once.

- When you have completed this program, select the meditations that resonated with you, that felt right for you. You do not have to do every meditation in this program to achieve your desires. However, you will not know if these medications are right for you unless you actually do them.

- Once you have selected the meditations that resonate with you, practice at least one of them each day. Meditation is about being still and quiet. Its purpose is to increase our awareness of the nature of the mind.

The goal of this program is not to eliminate unpleasant thoughts or emotions. The goal is to take charge of your mind. By learning to manage your thoughts and emotions, you will gain the upper hand. With time, the thoughts and emotions that you find to be problematic will naturally lose their potency. This is the end of this program; we wish you happiness and inner peace.

9 781801 347358